STRONG MEN DANGEROUS TIMES

Five Essentials Every Man Must Possess to Change His World

JIM RAMOS

COPYRIGHT

Five
Stones
Press

STRONG MEN
DANGEROUS
TIMES

Five Essentials Every Man Must Possess to Change His World

JIM RAMOS

CONTENTS

FOREWORD

I still remember the first time I met Jim Ramos. My dear friend and colleague in ministry, Rev. Gary McCusker, introduced him to me and shared their story as we sat around my conference table one afternoon. I was struck as I listened to how God had used Gary in Jim's life, both to bring him to Christ as well as to set for him an example in life and ministry. At the time Jim was serving as a youth pastor in Oregon, carrying on the legacy Gary had left and patterning his personal and professional life after that of his mentor. It reminded me of my relationship with my grandfather.

I have always been passionate about intergenerational ministry. Primarily because I believe it is the way the Christian faith is passed down from one generation to the next. I have experienced it in my own life as my grandfather poured his legacy into me, and I have seen it in the lives of people like Gary and Jim who have made such an impact for Christ and His Kingdom in the world.

Perhaps that's why I found myself listening with growing excitement as Jim unpacked a new vision God had placed on his life. Jim knew God was calling him to reach men. Old men. Young men and boys who had yet to reach manhood. Jim felt a calling from God to gather these men together across the generational spectrum, help them build deep friendships, and challenge them to spur one another on to growth in Christ.

He had gotten a taste of this in his own ministry to students as he watched some of them connect with older and wiser Christians in his church, but he desired to take this vision out beyond the bounds of youth ministry and reach the wider church through men. I loved the vision. I loved Jim's passion. But I will freely admit I was stunned when Jim left his position as youth pastor and went "all-in" to develop The Great Hunt for God, now called Men in the Arena! And I can't tell you how glad I am now that he did!

As a church, we have been privileged to have front row seats to what God is up to in The Great Hunt for God. During that initial year, Jim met with many men in our church to tease out and pray over his ideas. He led our annual Men's Getaway, which allowed him to further refine the vision God had laid on his heart and develop the principles that form the bedrock of the ministry.

I got to watch him in action as he taught our men how to protect their integrity, fight apathy, pursue God passionately, lead courageously, and finish strong. After each session, I observed the impact on our men as they wrestled with what God was saying to them through Jim. It was exciting to see God on the move that weekend! Towards the end of the retreat, as Jim continued to share his heart, we felt led by the Spirit to lay hands on him and commission him for this great work. It was a special moment for all of us!

From there, many of our men got involved in the ministry. Some became financial supporters. Others, like Gary McCusker, were asked to serve on the board. Our church became a Pioneering Church, financially supporting the movement. And over the years, I have watched Men in the Arena groups spring up in the life of our church with great impact.

I have had men share with me how being part of Men in the Arena has helped them see Jesus in new ways, saved their marriages, delivered them from sexual temptation and sin, made them better fathers, or changed their relationship with their own fathers.

They have shared with me how it has given them a passion to mentor younger men or find an older man to mentor them. They have told me how valuable it has been to be in groups that are intentionally intergenerational as we all seek to learn from one another what it means to die to self and follow Christ.

From the earliest days of the ministry where it was just Jim and a couple of banners and what he shared from his heart on retreats, to the development of resources such as *The Playbooks* and *The Field Guide (A Bathroom Book for Men),* to the launching of small groups of men who commit to grow deeper in relationship with each other and with Christ. God has clearly been at work using Men in the Arena for His purposes and glory!

As the senior pastor of our church, I judge success by one measure alone. Are we fulfilling the call of the Great Commission to make disciples? I ask this question each year when we evaluate the programs and ministries of our church. It guides everything we do. When it comes to Men in the Arena, I can confidently say that our men are becoming more faithful followers of Jesus. Can there be any greater praise?

Soli Deo Gloria,
Rev. Dr. Doug Resler
Senior Pastor
Parker Evangelical Presbyterian Church
Parker, Colorado

STRONG MEN DANGEROUS TIMES

Five Essentials Every Man Must Possess to Change His World

AN INTRODUCTION TO MANHOOD

PART I

THE TRAILHEAD: PROTECTING INTEGRITY

MAN LAW VIOLATIONS: A CONFUSED GENERATION

MAN LAW VIOLATIONS

A Confused Generation

"The ultimate measure of a man is not where he stands in moments of comfort and convenience, but where he stands at times of challenge and controversy."
~Martin Luther King, Jr.

So you too, when you do all the things which are commanded you, say, "We are unworthy slaves; we have done only that which we ought to have done."
~Luke 17:10

"A man must be big enough to admit his mistakes, smart enough to profit from them, and strong enough to correct them."
~John C. Maxwell

WANTED: STRONG MEN

What is a strong man? What does he do that makes him so? How is he different from his weaker male counterparts? What does it mean to be masculine in a society where phrases like, "toxic masculinity", "identify as male", and "bio

3

dad" are common vernacular? The bottom line is this: men are more confused than ever about what a man is, let alone what a strong man is. This book boldly defines what a strong man is and dispels all misconceptions about what a man is not.

According to Google the word *strong* has a dual meaning. First, *strong* is defined as "having the power to move heavy weights or perform other physically demanding tasks." Strong is also defined as being "able to withstand great force or pressure." Combining them, a *strong man* is one who **will** 1) carry heavy burdens, 2) withstand great pressures, and 3) move threatening obstacles, tangible or intangible, that threaten those in his sphere of influence. I say *will*, not *can*, because a strong man is willing and able to do each of the three when his masculinity is called upon. Weak men **can** do these three as well, but choose to neglect one or all of them for unknown reasons. Choice and habit separate the strong man from his weaker counterparts.

That being said, this book is more about scratching my own itch than anything else. I've been on a quest to understand manhood for decades. Let's be really honest. Our society, especially men, is softer than any other time in history. In affluent countries like America, it's even worse. Men are weaker than ever. The lines of manhood are blurred like no other time in history. The goal of this book is to help you understand manhood. Even more, I want the men I care the most deeply about—my sons—to be transformed as men.

These are dangerous times to be a man. Weaklings need not apply. Our world is quick to point the finger at males as the problem, which is true. Males have been, and are, the source of most of the world's problems. Countless amounts of resources, however, have been mistakenly dumped into fixing the symptoms not the cause. Symptoms like sex trafficking, fatherlessness, divorce, and violence would be eradicated if we focused on fixing the root problems and stop trying to stick a Band-Aid on the symptom. If you want to solve most of the world's problems—if males are indeed the source of most of them—the only logical solution is found in transforming males into men.

Why can't we see that?

Our world desperately needs strong men. Men who will carry the heavy weight of masculinity to a world that is desperate for them to step up. Masculinity is under attack like never before, and the blame can be laid at the feet of **weak males** masquerading as **strong men**. But the two couldn't be further apart. Similar in form, male is a different species altogether than a man in regard to function. A man is as a man does, not what he boasts or how he looks.

Young males today are confused. Heck, old ones are too! I'm often confused about what a man is and does. We throw the word "man" around so flippantly that it's come to describe a physically mature male. This couldn't be further from the truth. Men are confused. In an effort to understand manhood we've actually developed certain "man laws" and subsequent violations. Violating one of these sacred man laws threatens having your man card (whatever that is) revoked! Have you ever heard, "Hey, that's a man law violation!"? Or, "Hand over your man card"?

I have.

Check out some of these "Man Laws" that I've heard, or used, over the years. They illustrate our confusion about what a man is and does and how we've dealt with it in recent years. Enjoy!

A Man Law I'll die to avoid violating is what I call the **Proximity Law**. The Proximity Law states that a man should leave an open space between himself and the man next to him at urinals or any seat, especially the bench seat of your truck! In fact, even if you are the only guy in the bathroom, prepare for this by taking the outside-most urinal. If there are three, for example, leave the middle one open. This doesn't put another man in a compromising situation if he walks in while you're doing your business!

The Toasting Law is simply this: if you're having a beer with some buddies, celebrating at a wedding reception, or anywhere your team is winning—never toast with the rim of the bottle, glass, or Mason jar. Man, that's like kissing another dude!

While we're being politically incorrect, let's discuss the **Umbrella Law.** Men don't share umbrellas! Shoot, in the northwest where I live, men don't even use umbrellas! Men also don't share their everyday clothing or go to the bathroom together (why women do this is a mystery). While we're at it, don't ask me to get on the back of your motorcycle with you! My hands will never touch your waistline unless it's a life or death situation!

Also, you can firmly shake my hand, high-five, fist pound, and even chest bump me. But if you hug me, you have no more than three seconds—I'll be tapping 1-2-3—before you break the **Three Second Law**!

Selfie Law? Nope. Don't do it *unless* your wife, mother, or a child makes you take one with them. One exception to the Selfie Law is if you're ever in a situation similar to a good friend of mine. He shot a Mountain Goat in Wyoming and was miles from the closest human. But even then, he apologized for it!

Here are some **Social Media Laws** we must acknowledge. Never "poke" me, or invite me to Farmville, Candy Crush Saga, or any other child's game! Oh yeah, and no emojis—ever!

Let's get personal. I'm proud to be a bald man. But don't think that by rubbing my bald head, I might grant you three wishes. The only thing you'll receive by rubbing my perfectly round head is a head butt to the nose! Just kidding. Maybe.

Lastly, here's a Man Law violation that happens every week in churches around the world. I call this my **Lyrics Law.** Send a message to those pastors and worship leaders who insist on ignoring men in church budgets, teachings, and worship lyrics. Don't sing the girl parts. Protest any song with a la-la, whoop-whoop or oh-oh by staying silent. Never sing words to God that you wouldn't say to a buddy. Protest lyrics like this popular song, *"Your love is extravagant/Your friendship/it is intimate/I feel I'm moving to the rhythm of your grace/Your fragrance is intoxicating in the secret place, cause your love is extravagant."* What!?

Another notorious song lyric heard in churches all over America is, *"Heaven meets earth like a sloppy wet kiss."* Don't you dare try to kiss me bro. I don't want to smell your fragrance or move to any rhythm your body produces! Please show me one verse in the Word of God that supports this garbage. I dare you. I actually witnessed one of these songs at a large men's event! A men's event!

It was the last year of that event. Church leaders wonder why strong men would rather go to the mountains on Sunday to think about God than sit in their effeminate church thinking about the mountains! Now you know. We must figure this out if we want to attract strong men to our churches.

I'm not politically correct—neither is this book. Put it down if you're offended.

With all the confusion today how does a boy know when he's crossed over to manhood? Is it when he gets into his first fight? Maybe it's when he loses his virginity? Is he a man when he marries, can legally vote, drink, or fight for his country? Do you think he's a man when he gets his first job, or driver's license?

Better yet, what is a man? Does pubic hair make him a man? Does fathering a child make him a man? Is the rich, powerful, or successful guy a man? How about a professional athlete, famous actor, or high-level politician? What about Chuck Norris? Is he a man?

Probably.

Where does a young man learn about being a man? Does he learn it from his dad, respected coach, or pastor? Does he learn by watching television or the movies? Can he YouTube or Google it?

Strong Men Dangerous Times is a book that answers the question, "What is a man?" This book is written for the average man. It's short, simple, and to the point. It shouldn't take long to read through its pages. Put it on the back of your toilet seat and read a few pages each morning when you sit down. In a few weeks you'll have finished one of this generation's most transformative books about manhood.

Strengthen Your Grip
Chapter 1 Small Group Exercise

John C. Maxwell is credited with saying, "A man must be big enough to admit his mistakes, smart enough to profit from them, and strong enough to correct them." What does this say to you about strong men?

According to Google the word "strong" has a dual meaning. First, *strong* is defined as "having the power to move heavy weights or perform other physically demanding tasks." Strong is also defined as being "able to withstand great force or pressure." Combining them, a *strong* man is one who **will** carry heavy burdens, withstand great pressures, and move threatening obstacles, tangible or intangible, that threaten those in his sphere of influence.

In Luke 17:10 Jesus said, "So you too, when you **do** all the things which are commanded you, say, 'We are unworthy slaves; we have done only that which we ought to have done.'" What are some things strong men **do** that weak men defer?

Of the "Man Laws" mentioned in Chapter 1, which resonated with you? What other Man Laws can you think of? How do the Man Laws we live by speak to us about how confused men are about their masculinity?

AIM SMALL, MISS SMALL
The Patriot

"What did I tell you fellas about shooting?" Benjamin Martin
"Aim small, miss small." Nathan and Samuel Martin
"Aim small, miss small. Boys, Samuel, steady."
~Benjamin Martin
Movie, The Patriot

Be on the alert, stand firm in the faith, act like men, be strong.
~1 Corinthians 16:13

"A shepherd must tend his flock. And at times fight off the wolves."
~The Reverend,
Movie, The Patriot

Aim Small

"Aim small, miss small."

Who can forget that famous line from the 2000 movie *The Patriot*? It takes place in 1776 during the Revolutionary War as South Carolina farmer, widower, and legendary war hero Benjamin Martin (Mel Gibson) finds himself thrust into the war after helplessly watching his family torn apart. Unable to remain silent after one son, Thomas, is ruthlessly gunned down, another son, Gabriel, is hauled off to be hanged, and his plantation is set ablaze, Benjamin takes matters into his own hands.

Rushing into his burning home, Benjamin grabs all the weapons he can salvage, rallies his remaining young sons, Nathan and Samuel, and runs to cut off the Redcoats. The classic scene takes place on a knoll overlooking the wooded road. The footsteps of the approaching Redcoats can be heard under the trees as Benjamin hands each of his petrified sons a musket and calmly says, "What did I tell you fellas about shooting?"

Older brother Nathan and little brother Samuel reply, "Aim small, miss small."

. . .

Benjamin gives a few strategic instructions, smiles and says, "Aim small, miss small. Boys, Samuel, steady."

You have to watch the scene to truly appreciate what happens next.

But what you don't know is that while teaching Mel Gibson how to shoot a muzzle-loading rifle, technical advisor Mark Baker gave them the advice to "aim small, miss small," meaning that if you aim at a man and miss, you miss the man. But if you aim at a smaller object like a button and miss, you still hit the man. Gibson liked his advice so much he incorporated it into the ambush scene, and the rest is cinematic history.

Somewhere between the Victorian Era of the late 1800's, Industrial Revolution of the early 1900's, and the Feminist Movement of the mid 1900's, men have lost their way. No one's to blame for this demise but now is the time for us to reclaim our lost identity.

The original title of this book was *Aim Small, Miss Small* because a strong man needs a target that clearly defines manhood. The title was strategically changed to *Strong Men, Dangerous Times* because men need a target to measure their strength against. It's like the young mother of three daughters who shared, "Finally, my daughters have a dad to measure all men against." This a maximum impact book for men who want a target to zero in on their masculine aspirations.

Men are conquerors searching for the next hill to die on, goal to achieve, or target to shoot. Men lose heart when they lose sight of the target and settle into a mundane form of life that isn't really living. Once strong men become weak, and weak men remain so. About these men, Tony Compolo said, "Instead of praying, 'If I die before I wake,' we should pray, 'if I wake before I die!'"

Men come to life by giving themselves to a mission or purpose—a goal to conquer rather than being kicked or mocked when they're down. That's the purpose of this book. It will fill your lungs with life as you discover what a strong man is and does.

Yes! Life!

And yes, we've been so bold as to lay claim to the definition of manhood. This book contains five manhood essentials that every man must possess so his world, circle of influence, will feel the full weight of his masculine strength. No matter who you are, what you believe, where you came from, what hair color you have, or how much money you earn, *Strong Men, Dangerous Times* is for all who aspire to have maximum impact on their world. This book will keep you out of the anonymous bleachers and in the arena where you belong. This book takes a shot at manhood and hits the bullseye. So will your life once you understand and embrace your full capacity as a man. Like the saying goes, "If you aim at nothing, you'll hit it every time." Such has been the weakening of modern men, which will be eradicated by the end of the dangerous book in your hands.

Do you want life? Do you want to wake up before you die? Do you want to take a shot at understanding manhood? Then join me on the great adventure of understanding what it means to be a man.

Strengthen Your Grip
Small Group Exercise

In the movie *The Patriot*, the Reverend made a powerful statement, "A shepherd must tend his flock. And at times fight off the wolves." What are the wolves in your life and why do you need strength to battle them?

The original title of this book was *Aim Small, Miss Small* because a strong man needs a target that clearly defines manhood. The title was strategically changed to *Strong Men, Dangerous Times* because men need a reference point, a target to measure their strength against. In one sentence, how would you define manhood and why?

1 Corinthians 16:13-14 says, "Be on the alert, stand firm in the faith, act like men, be strong. Let all that you do be done in love." Which of these five things do you wrestle with the most and why?

Tony Compolo once said, "Instead of praying, 'If I die before I wake,' we should pray, 'if I wake before I die!'" Where do you need to wake up?

EVOLUTION OF MAN
The Definition of Manhood

"We have not men fit for the times. We are deficient in genius, in education, in gravity, in fortune, in everything."
~John Adams, 1774

That which has been is that which will be, and that which has been done is that which will be done. So there is nothing new under the sun.
~Ecclesiastes 1:9

"Nothing is true that is new, and nothing is new that is true."
~John Wesley

Origins

Robert Lewis introduced me to the qualifications of manhood with his book *The Raising of a Modern Day Knight*. I was forty-two years old, married, and raising three young sons. I'd never given much thought to manhood as an action or description. I'd considered a man to be any biologically mature male, but that changed when Lewis defined manhood by saying a man, "Accepts responsibility, rejects passivity, leads courageously, and expects a greater reward." Lewis' description inspired me to have a similar phrase engraved on three matching knives that I presented to my sons for Christmas.

When we launched Men in the Arena and began writing our curriculum using this engraved definition of manhood as an outline, I realized it fell tragically short and needed more. But what was missing? It didn't fully capture what a man is and does. Our definition of strong manhood didn't extend deep enough. The progressive verb tenses added to our a-man-is-as-a-man-does conviction, but our four components of manhood lacked punch, were too passive, and incomplete.

I loved the phrase "**rejecting passivity**", but it was too, uh, passive. Strong men don't draw a line in the sand and passively dare you to cross it. Strong men are interlopers who cross the lines their adversaries draw, push back darkness, and take new ground. Strong men do more than stand and reject. Strong men take the offensive whenever possible. See the dilemma? Furthermore, passivity is the fruit of the greater evil that the Bible calls callousness—also known as apathy or indifference (Isaiah 6:9-10). It's the heart hardening of one who has lost the will to resist the forces pushing against him—lost the will to fight. It's when a man stops caring about what he should have deep feelings for. Like losing a tug-of-war match, it's a picture of a weakened man being pulled over the line and failing to hold his ground.

"**Accepting responsibility**" was another problematic phrase. It was poetic when teamed with "rejecting passivity" but didn't hit the root of the problem. At the heart of a man who rejects responsibility is something much deeper—a lack of integrity. We've all known men who were once honorable men of integrity who got comfortable, lowered their guardrails, and fell victim to sin with a massive breach in their integrity. I don't care who you are or what you believe, if you lack integrity, you lack everything needed to be a man respected by other men as well as those who know you the most—your family.

Integrity must be protected every day, at all costs.

We adjusted our sights, anchored our focus, and hit the bullseye with the five-fold definition of manhood that make up the following sections of *Strong Men, Dangerous Times*: **protecting integrity, fighting apathy, pursuing God passionately, leading courageously, and finishing strong.**

Sometimes we make things too churchy. Whether you agree or not, the five strong man essentials needed to be true for those inside as well as outside the church walls. For many of my family and friends who don't attend church, don't consider themselves religious, and aren't vocal followers of Jesus—the Strong Man Essentials needed to strike a chord. It would need to cross religious, racial, generational, and geographic boundaries. Though I'm an outspoken follower of Jesus Christ, anyone boasting that they crafted a definition of manhood for **all men** couldn't limit it to men who attend church or believed a certain way.

Strong Men Dangerous Times had to be the most **definitive** work on manhood. And it is.

This became apparent a few years later while sitting in a hot tub with my brother Tom. Tom hasn't been a regular churchgoer since childhood, but he's a good man with a strong sense of honor, responsibility, and most of all, honesty. I knew he wouldn't pull any punches. He never does.

In that hot tub I put the "five essentials" to the test. Knowing Tom hadn't attended church in years I recited the five by memory and zeroed in on the third, "pursuing God passionately." Then I asked, "Tom, do you believe in God? Do you believe He made you? Do you believe He loves you? Do you believe He has a special mission for your life?"

"Bro, of course I do. You know that."

"Then", I reasoned, "How can you ever be the man you've been designed **by God** to be, apart from radical devotion to Him? You will never fully understand your life's purpose until you understand and have a relationship with the God who created you."

Through the mist of the spa I thought I saw his lips quiver. Tom gently set his beer on the deck, blew the smoke from his cigar, and said, "Bro, you're absolutely right."

That was the night the Strong Man Essentials every man must possess to change his world was born.

Strengthen Your Grip
Small Group Exercise

In 1774 John Adams said, "We have not men fit for the times. We are deficient in genius, in education, in gravity, in fortune, in everything." What "deficiencies" do others see in you? What are you doing about it?

Ecclesiastes 1:9 says, "That which has been is that which will be, and that which has been done is that which will be done. So there is nothing new under the sun." What new thing did you learn about manhood from this chapter and how will you apply it?

Strong Men Dangerous Times is divided into five essentials every man must possess to change his world. Those five essentials are: **protecting integrity, fighting apathy, pursuing God passionately, leading courageously, and finishing strong**. Which of these five is the most important for any man seeking to live as his best version?

Which of these do you question? Which do you struggle the most to put into practice?

We will go into great detail unpacking these five essentials in the coming chapters of the book. Hang on for the ride of your life!

MOVING TARGETS
What a Man Is Not

"Real manhood differs from simple anatomical maleness, that it is not a natural condition that comes about spontaneously through biological maturation but rather is a precarious or artificial state that boys must win against powerful odds."
~David Gilmore

When I was a child, I used to speak like a child, think like a child, reason like a child; when I became a man, I did away with childish things.
~1 Corinthians 13:11

"Manhood is something you earn. One coin at a time."
~David Murrow

Myths of Manhood

I grew up gun spoiled. I admit it. Dad was a high school teacher and coach most of his adult life, but he loved to buy and sell guns as a hobby. I say hobby because Dad rarely profited from buying and selling personal firearms.

During his lifetime he has bought, sold, or traded more guns than I can remember. When he bought a gun he really liked, it ended up with his children or grandchildren before he traded it for another. For example, Dad's all-time favorite rifle is the pre-1964 Winchester Model 70, chambered in .270 caliber. Guess what Dad gifted each of my sons as their first hunting rifle? Correct.

His favorite shotgun is the Winchester Model 12 first made in 1912. Guess what sits in my gun safe as a college graduation gift? Yep. Did I mention that I'm gun-spoiled?

For those reading who are not gun enthusiasts, let me explain the difference between shotguns and rifles. A rifle shoots a single bullet at high velocity over greater distances. To accomplish this it uses different gunpowder, encased in a highly resistant metal case—usually brass—and requires a thicker barrel. It is "rifled" with a spiral groove inside the full length of the barrel so the bullet spins, sending it spiraling point-first in an accurate trajectory over long distances.

Shotguns, conversely, shoot multiple spheres—called shot—over much shorter distances with an effective distance of no more than eighty yards (unless you're a storyteller). Shotgun barrels are thinner, not rifled, and are typically wider at the end depending on the type of shotgun. All things being equal with a particular shotgun, these barrel widths vary in diameter based on the "choke". Newer shotguns come with adjustable chokes you can use for varying shooting situations.

Generally speaking, hunters only shoot shotguns when pursuing game birds. To shoot a rifle at a game bird would be not only ludicrous and ineffective, but illegal! A bird hunter will use the shotgun every time, sending the shot in a spreading pattern.

Why?

Because game birds are usually moving and, other than turkeys, they're flying! Some birds are faster than others, some fly higher than others, and some come at different angles than others. You never know where a game bird will come from, where it will go, the exact speed it will fly, or what distance away it will be. What you do know is that it will be moving, and moving fast.

I've hunted game birds since youth, and I can tell you one thing that was as true for me then as it is for me today. **It's hard to hit a moving target.**

Men today live under gray skies. Black and white has faded, and men are confused about who they are and what they should do. This confusion has weakened them. Confusion leads to indecision and hesitation, but the strong man knows who he is. Contemporary illusions portrayed daily in the media make understanding manhood like hitting a moving target.

This is the era of the weak male. Our participation-trophy-culture has created entitled and impotent men who have nothing to offer besides intellectual excuses that fall sadly short of true strength. Spiritual leaders in too many churches have presented an effeminate version of Jesus that fits into their callous-free lives, protected from the real world behind a solid core door and administrative assistants who guard them like a pit bull from all potential interlopers. The Jesus they serve from the safety of their church office is nowhere near the Jesus we read about in Scripture who turned over tables, quieted raging storms, and nicknamed his three closest friends the Sons of Thunder and the Rock!

No wonder men are confused! No wonder they are weaker than ever.

Before I address the five Strong Man Essentials, let's look at what a strong man is not. Read carefully as I expose several myths of manhood that will destroy all false paradigms you have about manhood.

First, **manhood is not defined by a job or title.** What's the first question after every introduction between men?

"What do you do?"

Men, your career is not who you are. With the urbanization of America during the Industrial Revolution of the early 1900's people flocked to the cities and women entered the workforce in a non-agrarian role. In the past one hundred years, we've moved from a traditional family structure to a more egalitarian model where spouses share the work and household loads. This has created confusion for men, who for centuries identified who they were as men with what they did. In many households, not only does the wife work, she's the primary wage earner. Can you see how this impacts a man's identity?

Second, **manhood is not defined by social status or financial portfolio.** The ability to make money and the ability to act as a man are different. We wrongly assume that the rich somehow have it together but it's often quite the opposite. Think about the 22-year-old who is a multimillionaire simply because he can run fast, jump high, or throw a ball accurately. To think that young male is a man because he can afford an agent diminishes what manhood really is.

Wealth and status make it easier to cover deeper issues and hide them behind the cloud of money. Think about the rich and famous. Do they have it together? Do movie stars we watch live like the characters they portray in the movies they make? No, because it's fiction! In real life, most are nothing more than dressed up train wrecks.

Let me throw another truth into the mix. Did I mention that Jesus was never elevated in Scripture because of his great carpentry skills? Did you know that Jesus was strategically homeless for at least three or four years of his life? He said of himself, *"Foxes have dens and birds have nests, but the Son of Man has no place to lay his head" (Matthew 8:20).* Clearly, wealth does not mean that one man is stronger than another.

Third, **manhood is not defined by talents or abilities.** When vacationing in Mexico we ran into a newlywed couple poolside. I soon learned that the husband worked for a professional baseball scouting company, specializing in pitchers. I knew in college football what separates a Division I from a Division III athlete is not heart, skill, or intelligence. It's often simply a game of metrics—height, weight, and speed. I had noticed that most Major League Baseball pitchers are tall, and have a long arm and stride. I asked him if similar metrics applied for baseball and he not only affirmed my assumption, but also took it to the next level.

"We actually use a mathematical equation based on arm length, stride, and height. We can determine with a high level of accuracy the maximum output (speed) potential of a young pitcher. If he's too short, for example, we will barely give him a look because his maximum output won't be high enough. It's a metrics game. Drive and determination have little to do with our recruiting. Everyone has that."

Think about this. If your metrics are exceptional along with throwing accuracy, you can be a 20-year-old millionaire who is on television commercials, is famous, and has thousands of fans cheering every time you step on the mound.

But it doesn't make you a man. The genetics to meet a mathematical standard and throw an accurate 100-mile-an-hour fastball only makes you a good pitcher. It just means you can throw things fast, accurate, and make a lot of money.

Your family, friends, and God are way more in need of a good man than they are of good metrics!

Next, **manhood is not defined by a specific age** either. Chronology does not equate to manhood. Action does. A man is as a man does. Almost daily I witness forty, fifty, and sixty-year-old men who are males but not men. They are boys masquerading in a man's body. A while back, a man entered a building without his wife and I wondered out loud, "I haven't seen his wife with him lately."

The 80-year-old man next to me matter-of-factly stated, "He's divorcing her because she's a slob. Do you blame him?"

"Yes I do! He's a male but not a man and neither are you for making that comment," I restrained myself from saying.

Manhood is not defined by anatomy. Just as reaching the age of pubic hair does not turn a male into a man neither does having a penis make you a man. Men aren't born. Babies are born. Children are raised. But men, oh men, they're forged in the fires of responsibility, compounded daily over time. A man is made. And after he's been made, a man acts like a man.

Lastly, and the most importantly, **manhood is not defined by "looking" like a man**. Let me explain. A strong man is not about his image, it's about his action. Have I said this before? We have a hugely mistaken stereotype that a man is built, talks, and dresses a certain way. Just because he is built like a bodybuilder, wears a flannel with his jeans and boots, drives a big truck, and swings an ax for a living means nothing. Some of the weakest, most childish men I know have looked like "tough guys". I have a suggestion for all you tough guys out there. Stop trying to act like a strong man and start living like one.

Strengthen Your Grip
Small Group Exercise

This chapter was introduced with an illustration about using shotguns to hit moving targets. What moving targets have you been taught about manhood that are not Biblically true. How do you identify and eradicate these myths from your life?

David Gilmore is quoted saying, "Real manhood differs from simple anatomical maleness in that it is not a natural condition that comes about spontaneously through biological maturation but rather is a precarious or artificial state that boys must win against powerful odds." What do you think he meant? How is maturation into manhood a "precarious" state that young men do battle for against "powerful odds"?

Near the end of the "Love Chapter" in 1 Corinthians 13:11 the Apostle Paul wrote, "When I was a child, I used to speak like a child, think like a child, reason like a child; when I became a man, I did away with childish things." How do speaking, thinking and reasoning change when an immature male grows into a man?

Which of these three—speaking, thinking, reasoning—needs the most attention from you and why? What blind spots might you be missing?

HONEYMOON FROM HELL
Males are Born, Men are Made

"It takes one to know one."
~Idiom

Husbands, love your wives, just as Christ also loved the church and gave Himself up for her, so that He might sanctify her, having cleansed her by the washing of water with the word, that He might present to Himself the church in all her glory, having no spot or wrinkle or any such thing; but that she would be holy and blameless.
~Ephesians 5:25-27

"The American male is in a fundamental struggle for his identity."
~Weldon Hardenbrook
Missing from Action

Yosemite

My 22-year-old bride Shanna married a 26-year-old male. But he was not a strong man, even though he looked the part. She married a boy masquerading as a man. He looked good on paper, having all the required masculine credentials. He played college football. He benched 400 pounds. He wore Wranglers. He was an outdoorsman. He was a football coach. He was a pastor. He had a college education. He—I—was weak in so many areas and had so much to learn about true—masculine—strength.

I joke now that I married an angel and woke up with Satan. Shanna reciprocates that she married her dream guy but woke up in a nightmare. Maybe if she married a stronger man, things would have been better.

Our marriage started on the wrong foot and got worse. Working full time as a Youth for Christ/Campus Life Director meant we were broke. For our honeymoon someone gave us the ingenious idea to go to Yosemite National Park. So we borrowed her parents' camper and drove away with (thanks to her sister) a hand-scribbled poster taped on the back that read, "If this campers rockin', don't bother knockin'!"

. . .

Between the bear almost running me over in camp, Europeans who insisted on hiking the wrong side (left) of the trail, waiting thirty minutes for a public shower, and my sweet bride destroying me in cards (I still accuse her of cheating), we were exhausted and wondering if we made the right decision to marry after only nine months of dating.

We were committed. But not too convinced.

"No worries," I ignorantly thought. "Everything will change once we get home."

Oh, was I wrong! On our first night in our apartment I asked Shanna what was for dinner, and she pointed to the cabinet and sweetly said, "I don't cook, but I think there's Top Ramen in the cupboard."

She doesn't cook?

"Okay, wanna have sex?" I figured now that we were married, and it was okay in God's eyes I'd get sex on demand. Well, I wanted her...now! Man, was I wrong!

Denied, shocked, and starving, I decided to take a nap in a gloriously made bed. You must understand that I hadn't slept in a bed with sheets and a comforter in years. Instead, for the previous seven years, I slept in two sleeping bags zipped together and thrown on a mattress. So you can imagine the horror when I went to rest on one of the eight glorious pillows and a fluffy down comforter and was told to use my stained old college pillow because the others were "decorative"!

I took a brief nap on a smelly college pillow, went to shower, and was told not to touch the new forest green and navy-blue wedding towels perfectly folded over the towel bar, because they too were, yep, "decorative".

Things declined in our relationship to the point that after a year, I prayed on numerous occasions for God to take her out so I wouldn't have to divorce her. You read that correctly. I wanted her dead and asked God on numerous occasions to make it so.

I was almost 30. I was a devoted follower of Jesus. I was a pastor. I was a male but was far from a man. I was a weak man at best.

Two miserable years passed, we had our first son, and I was a youth pastor in a local church, but things hadn't changed much. It was 1995. We were committed to Jesus and each other. But we were struggling.

. . .

Things would soon change dramatically. Our church went to a Promise Keepers event with 70,000 men in the L.A. Coliseum. The speakers were amazing, and I connected with all of them—all but one.

One preacher came out in his full-length priestly robe and in the southern California heat screamed for what seemed like an hour the same phrase over and over (I may be exaggerating a little), "You've got to out love and out serve your wife!"

Turned off by his priestly apparel, the heat in the Coliseum, and his constant rant to "out love and out serve my wife", I checked out and began to read the event program.

Midway through his rant and all alone in that hot stadium, God spoke to me, as the obnoxious pastor clothed in all his glory shouted for the millionth time, "You've got to out love and out serve your wife!"

It hit me like a ton of bricks. I turned to the forgotten man next to me. "I just had an epiphany," I said. **"God just spoke to me. I need to out love and out serve my wife!"**

True story.

On that sweltering Southern California day, a 30-year-old man became a man. God began to transform me from a weak male to a strong man. When I returned, I publicly committed in front of our church to out love and out serve Shanna. Guess what, decades later I'm still doing it. The best part is that Shanna would agree.

Coincidentally, our marriage changed that day. Even more shocking is that soon after that event, my angry, complaining, nightmare of a wife changed into the person she is today—my best friend. Coincidence?

When a man gets it—everyone wins.

Men aren't born. They're made. I should know because it takes one to know one.

Strengthen Your Grip
Small Group Exercise

In the book, *Missing from Action*, Weldon Hardenbrook wrote, "The American male is in a fundamental struggle for his identity." What does he mean? How have you struggled with your identity? How do you see this struggle in other generations of men?

Ephesians 5:25-27 tells husbands to, "Love your wives, just as Christ also loved the church and gave Himself up for her, so that He might sanctify her, having cleansed her by the washing of water with the word, that He might present to Himself the church in all her glory, having no spot or wrinkle or any such thing; but that she would be holy and blameless." Where can you love your wife better? If you are single, what are you doing now to love your future wife?

In this chapter Jim told the story of the day he became a man at 30 years old when a preacher compelled him to, "Out love and out serve your wife!" What about his story resonates with you? Who out loves and out serves better, you or your wife?

The chapter ends with the Men in the Arena tagline, "When a man gets it—everyone wins." What is "it" and what does "it" look like? Is there an "it" that those closest to you are praying for you to get?

MACHO MACHO MAN
All Shapes and Sizes

"There are some, I rejoice to acknowledge, who will not be content with shallow logic. They will admit the force of the argument, and then turn away with tears to hunt (for) some lonely place and pray, 'O God, show me thy glory.' They want to taste, to touch with their hearts, to see with their inner eyes the wonder that is God."
~*A.W. Tozer*
The Pursuit of God

"Masculinity is not something given to you, but something you gain. And you gain it by winning small battles with honor."
~*Norman Mailer*

"Give me one hundred men who fear nothing but sin and desire nothing but God, and I care not whether they be clergyman or laymen, they alone will shake the gates of Hell and set up the kingdom of Heaven upon the earth."
~*John Wesley*

Cancun

In the last chapter you heard a little about what is known in Ramos family history as the "Honeymoon from Hell". We waited fifteen years for a hard-earned, real honeymoon—an all-inclusive trip to Cancun, Mexico with some close friends.

After a morning workout I took a shower before going to the pool. After getting dressed, I walked out to our eighth-story balcony to see if Shanna was at the pool. As I did, Village People's "Macho Man" began playing at the pool deck. In vacation mode, I quickly got Shanna's attention and began to lip-synch the words, doing my best to convince Shanna that she was married to a macho man, *"Hey, hey, hey, hey, hey. Macho, macho man. I gotta be a macho man.* **Macho macho man I gotta be a macho..."**

Unbeknownst to me, eight stories down Shanna was filming the whole thing! She has that video hidden to this day and I'm afraid for the day she uses it against me!

By now you should know the heart of this book is not about some macho, macho man. People question when I tell them what I do and the name of the organization we founded, Men in the Arena, "Is it some kind of macho organization for macho manly men only?"

"Not at all," I respond. "I consider myself a man's man, but this organization has nothing to do with some false pretenses surrounding some macho image. It has to do with men becoming their best version through Christ." Manhood is not about appearances. It's about action.

If there is anything I've learned about manhood it is this: men come in all shapes, sizes, colors, ages, and overall image. We must be careful to never judge a man based on his words or appearance but on his actions. Let me unpack this for you.

A redneck can be a man. A computer geek can be a man. A musician can be a man. A construction worker can be a man. A poet can be a man. A sportsman can be a man. A vegan can be a man. A carnivore can be a man. An athlete can be a man. An artist can be a man. A liberal can be a man. A conservative can be a man. A cat lover can be a man. A truck owner can be a man. And yes, a dude with a man bun, mullet, or comb-over (God help us) can be a man.

He can be short and round. He can be tall and thin. He can be muscular. He can be ugly, average, or good-looking. He can be an amputee, athlete, or average Joe. He can be bald, have a full head of hair, or rock the Cul De Sac (some call it the Horse Shoe or Landing Strip). He can have a mustache, goatee, beard, or can be clean-shaven.

He might be black. He might be white. He might be African, Indian, or Asian. He can be brown, yellow, red, white, and blue. Color does not make the man.

He might be a suit-wearing businessman in the city. He might be a jeans-wearing farmer in the country. He might be a khaki-wearing commuter in the suburbs, a shorts-wearing realtor on the west coast, or anything in between.

The bottom line is this– a man looks like many things and comes in many shapes and sizes, but at the end of the day manhood is about action. It's about the choices he makes more than any other non-essential aspect of manhood.

A man is as a man does.

Strengthen Your Grip
Small Group Exercise

John Wesley once said, "Give me one hundred men who fear nothing but sin and desire nothing but God, and I care not whether they be clergyman or laymen, they alone will shake the gates of Hell and set up the kingdom of Heaven upon the earth." What needs to happen for you to be numbered as one of the hundred men Wesley sought after?

What macho man images have you embraced that are actually false narratives about Biblical masculinity?

Jim wrote, "If there is anything I've learned about manhood it is this: men come in all shapes, sizes, colors, ages, and overall image. We must be careful to never judge a man based on his words or appearance but on his actions. Let me unpack this for you." How have you allowed artificial **forms** to precede actual functions of manhood?

What do you think about the statement that, "The bottom line is this– a man looks like many things and comes in many shapes and sizes, but at the end of the day manhood is about action. It's about the choices he makes more than any other non-essential aspect of manhood. A man is as a man does"? Can you identify an area where you need to worry less about your image and more about your actions?

Climbing The Mountain of Manhood
Manhood from the Summit

"Impossibilities vanish when a man and his God confront a mountain."
~Abraham Lincoln

And He said to them, "Because of the littleness of your faith; for truly I say to you, if you have faith the size of a mustard seed, you will say to this mountain, 'Move from here to there,' and it will move; and nothing will be impossible to you."
~Matthew 17:20

"We are in the position of travelers who, after surveying a great mountain from afar, traveling around it, and observing how it dominates the landscape and determines the features of the surrounding countryside, now approach it directly, with the intention of climbing it."
~J.I. Packer: Knowing God

The Strong Man

Manhood isn't easy. In fact, it's the most difficult thing a man will ever do. If it were easy, every male would be a man and every weak man would be strong. Manhood is a high and lofty goal because it's a daily choice. I can be a man today and do manly things, then revert into boyish behaviors tomorrow. If you don't believe me, just ask my wife!

If you really don't believe me, ask **your** wife!

The goal of *Strong Men, Dangerous Times* is to define what a man is and does in a world that has blurred the lines. This, you'll see, is the easy part. Any male can read this book but not just any man can live it out every day of his life. Like the Marines slogan, manhood belongs to the few, the proud.

Author and friend Bill Perkins wrote, "We live in a time of spiritually passive men who can't see that we've become spiritual jellyfish flowing with cultural norms."

I couldn't agree more.

Up to this point I've made a strong argument that manhood **is not** about age, appearance, abilities, anatomy, fame, status, or title. We do men a disservice by assuming they are strong men based only on these categories. A man is as a man does. It's really that simple.

Being called a man is a high compliment. Calling a male, or adult boy, a man is a punch in the groin to the real men out there. Let's start identifying men by their actions, not their anatomy. In this chapter we'll fly over manhood at 30,000 feet and offer an overview of the five essentials of manhood. They'll be expanded upon in the rest of the book, but you can put the book down after this chapter if you'd like and walk away, though you'd miss out on the deeper explanations of manhood and some awesome stories.

First, take note of the progressive form of each verb in the five characteristics of manhood. It is not by accident. The "ing" implies that manhood is a daily action. It's progressive. Manhood rests on how I live and the choices I make today. Yesterday's decisions are gone. They're history. They only exist in a memory. Only today matters to a man. I can act like a man today and revert to a male tomorrow.

A man is as a man does.

Every mountain climb starts at the trailhead. The trailhead up the mountain of manhood is "**protecting integrity**". In a nutshell, integrity is moral and ethical completeness. It's one's character traits fully matured and connected. It's the complete man. It's the man in all his strength—without fracture. It's the unbroken man.

I've never heard a strong man who raised his children to become dishonorable, worthless, lazy, liars, or criminals. Those are the teachings of weak and toxic men who we also call males. Instead, from very early on, strong men train their children to be honorable men of integrity. Regardless of your race or religion this is true.

Whether you're an atheist, agnostic, Muslim, Jew, Buddhist, Mormon, Hindu, or follower of Jesus, integrity is important. It's critical. It's foundational for manhood. This may sound contrary for some, but it's true, nonetheless. It's everything to be respected by one's peers. You can have everything but without integrity you've lost the starting point of manhood.

Integrity is the catalyst in the making of a man. It's the trailhead.

"**Fighting apathy**" is a bit more obscure than integrity but as we unpack it, you'll agree it's the greatest battle a man will ever fight. More than greed, selfishness, gossip, gluttony, or indebtedness, the fight against apathy exceeds them all. Apathy is a lack of feeling that anything really matters. It's indifference, like when the high school teacher asked her students to explain the difference between ignorance and apathy. One bored student half-heartedly turned to his buddy and said, "I don't know, and I don't care!"

I love it!

In the Bible the word most often associated with apathy is callousness. Callousness occurs when over time a part of the body becomes hardened and dulled to sensation. There are forces trying to pull men down as they climb. Sadly, effeminate churches, cultural norms, and subjective media dull us into passive apathy. Learn to relentlessly fight apathy at all costs!

The summit of manhood is "**pursuing God passionately**". A man is never stronger than when he passionately pursues his Creator. Biblical manhood can't be achieved without radical commitment to the Lord Jesus Christ. My stake is in the ground, the line is drawn in the sand, and I will die on this hill. You will never reach the summit of manhood, the apex of what it means to be a man, without radical devotion to your Creator. If you haven't already, give your life right now to the Creator of the Universe! He'll take you on the ride of your life!

Yes, you can be a man without Jesus. It would be ludicrous to think otherwise. You can be a good man without Jesus. You might even become a great man without Jesus. Let's be honest with each other for a moment. We both know a myriad of men who refuse to attend church or claim faith in Jesus who—for whatever reason—are far better men than most who do. We see it all the time.

We've all known or read about some real dirtbags who not only attended churches, they pastored them! Let's not be so naïve as to disregard this sad and embarrassing truth.

But hear me when I say this. You will never be the best version of you without radical surrender to the God who made you. Follow the simple logic. How will you ever become the best version of you without passionate devotion to the One who made you? Who else can lead you on the elusive path to your best self?

Forget about the churches that turned you off with their effeminate lyrics, flower-decorated platforms, and weak pastors who rarely venture beyond the safety of their holy hideouts. Jesus is a man's man. He willingly died the most horrible of deaths so you could live true life now. Now it's your turn to reciprocate with your life. Jesus will make you a stronger man than you ever imagined! He did it for me, and he'll do it for you.

The descent of manhood begins with what we call "**leading courageously**". After three decades of full-time ministry, one of the biggest problems I encountered wasn't the punch stains left in carpets, angry members, or the stupid things teens do (like taking Viagra on a mission trip to Mexico just to see what it would do). My biggest problems came from disengaged "Christian" dads who deferred spiritual leadership to their wives or the local church.

Reaching the summit of manhood means nothing if we relax and fail on the way down. According to science20.com, "Counterintuitively, most deaths (on Mt. Everest) occur on the *descent*, in the so-called Death Zone just above 8000 meters (about 26,000 feet)."

Why? One reason is because climbers lose their focus after they've achieved their summit goals and get careless on the descent. Should-be leaders see their should-be followers flounder disastrously when they set the wrong kind of example. They often bask in the glory of their past instead of leading in the present. But men lead courageously throughout their lives. They lead their families and other followers so that those they love can reach the new heights.

Strong men are committed to "**finishing strong**", which is the end of the trail —the end of life. However, weaker men are confused into believing that ending and finishing are synonymous. They are not. Quitting before a job is complete, being fired, or losing your marriage are wrong finishes, not strong ones. For example, divorce is an end of a marriage but not a finish. Suicide is an end of a life, but not the fulfillment of it. Getting fired is an end of a job but one that no strong man would be proud of.

Strong men are committed to finishing strong at all costs. Whether it be their workout, workday, or working on their marriage, strong men persevere with endurance and tenacity rather than finish weak. Males or weak men accept finishing wrong, but men settle for nothing less than finishing strong.

The next section will address the trailhead of masculinity as we climb and descend the mountain of manhood in this book. In the following chapter we'll take the path less traveled and look closely at five essentials every man must possess to change his world. Be forewarned that every climb involves resistance and pain. Strong men aren't born. They are made. They are forged in the fires of great pain and resistance.

Mentally prepare yourself to be challenged as you make the journey that only the strongest men are willing to endure.

Strengthen Your Grip
Small Group Exercise

Bill Perkins wrote, "We live in a time of spiritually passive men who can't see that we've become spiritual jellyfish flowing with cultural norms." When is this statement true about you? When are you at your weakest?

In this chapter the five essentials of manhood are explained using the progressive verb tense. Jim writes, "The 'ing' implies that manhood is a daily action. It's progressive. Manhood rests on how I live and the choices I make today. Yesterday's decisions are gone. They're history. They only exist in a memory. Only today matters to a man. I can act like a man today and revert to a male tomorrow." Which of the five essentials do you struggle with the most to form daily rhythms and habits?

We all know great men in history who never professed faith in Christ. We've also known of horrible men who were Christians and spiritual leaders. What are your thoughts about this sentence, "You will never be the **best version** of you without radical surrender to the God who made you"? Have you moved into the faith arena? What is stopping you from radically giving your life to Jesus and stepping into the best version of you?

In Matthew 17:20 Jesus said, "For truly I say to you, if you have faith the size of a mustard seed, you will say to this mountain, 'Move from here to there,' and it will move; and nothing will be impossible to you." What is faith? What does it look like? Where does your faith need to grow?

Kentucky Fried Integrity
Putting the Pieces Together

"Integrity is a commitment to say it, do it, live it."
~Bob Mason
Men in the Arena "Original 15"

*"Teacher," they said, "we know that you are a man of integrity and that you
teach the way of God in accordance with the truth. You aren't swayed by others,
because you pay no attention to who they are."*
~Matthew 22:16 (NIV)

*"I can get up off my chair with a smile on my face, and nobody will know there is
hatred in my Heart—the cesspool underneath my skin."*
~Henry Brandt

Character Versus Integrity

I heard a story about a married couple that headed to a secluded park for a picnic
date on a sunny Sunday afternoon. On their way they bought a box of chicken
from their favorite fast food restaurant. After ordering an eight-piece chicken
meal with biscuits, mashed potatoes, gravy, and coleslaw, they pulled out of the
parking lot and onto the highway. The wife checked the order, as wives often do,
but to her shock there was no chicken in the box! Instead she stared into a box
full of cash! They quickly returned to exchange the box full of money for their
eight-piece chicken meal.

When they finally arrived, the distraught manager was frantically searching
for a lost box of cash that had been misplaced at the shift change. The husband,
box in hand, approached the shift manager and explained the misunderstanding.

His job saved; the shift manager picked up the phone to call the local news
about this couple's great story of integrity!

Hearing this, the husband pulled the manager aside and whispered, "Hey
buddy, you can't do that. You can't call the news."

.   .   .

"Why not?" The shift manager explained, "I haven't seen such integrity in all my life. This is newsworthy for sure!"

Pointing at the beautiful woman in the passenger seat the man explained, "Do you see that good-looking woman sitting in that car over there? Truth be told, she's not my wife!"

He was a husband, all right! And she was a wife. The problem was, they weren't married to each other! Integrity is more than appearances. It's more than what we see. Integrity is who you are when nobody's watching. As the great American evangelist D.L. Moody once said, "Integrity is who you are in the dark."

Protecting integrity is the first of our five strong man essentials defining manhood. Integrity is the trailhead of manhood. It's the starting point for the weak man who aspires to ascend to a stronger level of manhood. It doesn't matter who you are or what you believe, if you lack this essential, you're missing the foundational component of manhood. The stronger the man, the stronger his foundation. For all strong men that foundation starts with protecting integrity. But before moving deeper into this section let's clarify two words that are often confused: character and integrity.

As you read the definition of **integrity** note its singularity. Where plural nouns describe and define character, integrity implies something single, whole, and complete. Integrity, according to *Merriam-Webster's Dictionary,* is "firm adherence to a code of values … the state of being *complete* or *undivided*."

Integrity is a man living at full capacity. It's the completed circle. Integrity is a man living as his best version. My close friend Rick would say it's the "full throttle man".

Now, let's take a look at the definition of character.

According to the *Merriam-Webster's Dictionary*, character is "the *complex* of mental and ethical *traits* marking and often individualizing a person, group, or nation." Notice the plurality of character. Character consists of many components —spiritual truth, work ethic, loyalty, honesty, fidelity, health, love, personal growth, and the list goes on and on.

Imagine the box of chicken in our opening story. Character represents the many pieces in the box of chicken. Each piece of chicken represents a characteristic—or trait—that marks an individual.

Let's say you are filling the box with a whole chicken, one piece at a time. Each piece matters to the completion of the box of chicken. Though many, the pieces fit together to form a complete bird; two thighs, two wings, two breasts, and two drumsticks. Each piece is essential to the box of chicken. If you buy a whole box of chicken and are missing just one piece, you will instantly recognize the breach of integrity, and will turn your car around, head back to KFC and make sure you get what you paid for. I know I would!

For the strong man lives a growth journey that ends at death (Philippians 1:6). He realizes that the breath in his lungs means he has purpose and meaning and that he must continue his growth journey for his integrity to remain whole. How does that growth happen? Like our t-shirt saying, "Males are born. Men are made". Men are being remade each day, every day. We lay claim to manhood daily. Manhood is a choice, and the choice to be a man is the decision to grow.

Integrity is the fruit of man's choices compounded over time. It can be lost. It can be forfeited. It can be compromised. What would the woman say who married a man of integrity, when years later that husband became a chronic adulterer? How about the orphaned child who has a sperm-donor-excuse for a dad? What about the sloth who refuses to honor his neighbors by maintaining his yard? Ask a man about a friendship that was destroyed by a backstabbing friend.

Don't stop at having a few solid character traits but strive to grow all of your essential traits into the wholeness of manly integrity.

Strengthen Your Grip
Small Group Exercise

What did you think of the statement that, "For all strong men, that foundation starts with protecting integrity?" How does poor character hinder the respect of those you work, live, and associate with?

Even Jesus' enemies acknowledged his integrity when they questioned, "Teacher," they said, "we know that you are a man of integrity and that you teach the way of God in accordance with the truth. You aren't swayed by others, because you pay no attention to who they are" (Matthew 22:16). Do your adversaries stand against you because of a cause you believe in or a breach in your integrity? How has your lack of integrity placed strain on any of your relationships?

Henry Brandt said, "I can get up off my chair with a smile on my face, and nobody will know there is hatred in my heart—the cesspool underneath my skin." Are you hiding a dark secret behind a bright smile? Is there bondage to sin, bitterness towards another, or a burden you are carrying that if you confessed it, would flood your life with light and freedom?

Jim wrote, "Integrity is the fruit of man's choices compounded over time. It can be lost. It can be forfeited. It can be compromised. What would the woman say who married a man of integrity, when years later that husband became a chronic adulterer? How about the orphaned child who has a sperm-donor-excuse for a dad? What about the sloth who refuses to honor his neighbors by maintaining his yard? Ask a man about a friendship that was destroyed by a backstabbing friend." Share about a time when your lack of integrity compounded until you had a train wreck experience.

LEANING
The Foundational Component of Manhood

"Children are not casual guests in our home. They have been loaned to us temporarily for the purpose of loving them and instilling a foundation of values on which their future lives will be built."
~James Dobson

Therefore everyone who hears these words of Mine and acts on them, may be compared to a wise man who built his house on the rock. And the rain fell, and the floods came, and the winds blew and slammed against that house; and yet it did not fall, for it had been founded on the rock. Everyone who hears these words of Mine and does not act on them, will be like a foolish man who built his house on the sand. The rain fell, and the floods came, and the winds blew and slammed against that house; and it fell—and great was its fall.
~Matthew 7:24-27

"Do you wish to rise? Begin by descending. You plan a tower that will pierce the clouds? Lay first the foundation of humility."
~Saint Augustine

The Tower of Pisa

The Tower of Pisa is known worldwide for its unintended tilt. It is 183 feet high from the ground on the low side, and 186 feet on the high side. The construction of the Tower of Pisa began on August 9, 1173, and was originally designed to be a bell tower. The tower stood upright for over five years, but just after the completion of the second floor, in 1178, it began to lean.

The foundation of the tower, only ten feet deep, was built on a dense clay mixture that was too soft to hold the tower upright. Because of its weight, the Tower sank downward until it had found the weakest point and began to lean in that direction. Construction halted for 100 years after the tower began to lean while the Italian government hoped the soil would settle, giving it enough strength to hold the weight of the tower.

The tilt remains, even though the structure was stabilized, but was partially corrected during the restoration work performed between 1990-2001. Prior to the restoration efforts the tower leaned at an angle of five-and-a-half degrees, but now leans just four degrees. In other words, the top of the tower is displaced horizontally twelve feet, ten inches from the center.

What a great example to illustrate integrity as the foundational component of manhood!

Foundations

The first of our five essentials, **protecting integrity**, was strategically placed ahead of the other strong man characteristics because it is the catalyst of manhood. It's the launch pad. It's the starting line. It's the trailhead for any man who longs to be a strong, powerful, man. I've met many men who claimed to follow Jesus but whose integrity was constantly in question. I've met many others who were openly irreligious, or practiced different religions, yet had tremendous integrity. Unlike the "Real Men Love Jesus" t-shirts that surfaced several years back, experience teaches, and the Bible confirms, that integrity *is not* a spiritual gift, fruit of the Spirit, or supernaturally imparted quality, but is developed over time by men who choose to actively live as the best version of themselves.

Even Jesus said, *"Therefore everyone who hears these words of Mine and acts on them, may be compared to a wise man who built his house on the rock" (Matthew 7:24).*

Did you catch that? Jesus said, "And acts on them." Building a firm foundation of integrity takes not only hearing the truth, but also *acting on it.* When we refuse to act with integrity on the things that we know are true, our foundation becomes unstable. It shifts. It moves. It oscillates.

Yes, it leans.

In other words, integrity is foundational for any male who aspires to manhood. We call this the *trailhead* because without integrity the journey towards manhood is stymied. It starts off in the wrong direction. Years ago, I decided to climb Mount Whitney in a day. At 14,505 feet above sea level, it is the tallest mountain in the contiguous United States. The climb involves 6,000 vertical feet of gain, 22 miles round trip, and 11-14 hours of hiking on average.

Our plan was to summit before the lightning storms that consistently hit in the early afternoon. This required us to leave our camp at Whitney Portals several hours before dawn. Headlamps burning a path, about an hour into the hike we made a wrong turn and were soon lost. Thankfully we corrected our error and found the main trail. Continuing down the wrong path could have cost us hours of much needed time to summit and descent before the summer thunderstorms.

Integrity is the trail strong men travel on. Any breach in integrity is a temporary detour down a toxic trail of weak masculinity. Some of those detours lead to deadly cliffs! During every moment when we lack integrity, we fall short of what is needed to be the strong man God originated. I can't stress *this enough:* Our journey as men hangs moment-by-moment, hour-by-hour, and day-by-day on our decision to live lives of integrity.

Think about it. The first virtues that good parents teach their children are qualities of integrity: honesty (tell the truth), generosity (share with others), courtesy (be nice to people), honor (pick up after yourself), and work ethic (do your chores). Parents teach these virtues because they know that integrity is foundational to growing into a contributing adult in society. Put into practice in your own life what you would preach to a child!

Leaning Lessons

The leaning Tower of Pisa is famous. It's notoriously renowned because of its poor foundation.

It's awkward.

It *leans.*

Buildings, like men, were made to **stand upright.** Tragically, we live in a culture dominated by weak males—bio dads, baby daddies, deadbeats, and absentee fathers (there's an oxymoron) are not only common terms today but are the accepted norm. The awkwardly leaning male masquerading as a strong man is in the majority, but a man who chooses the path of strength stands head and shoulders above the rest. Be that man!

Not only is the "leaning" Tower of Pisa awkward on the horizon, but even its name is identified by the lean. It's no longer addressed by its original name, the Tower of Pisa. Those who lack integrity over time are *identified* by their depravity.

"He's a liar."

"He's a cheater."

"He's a dead beat."

"He can't keep a job."

I don't know about you, but I'll think twice before standing under the leaning side of the tower. History has already proven the instability of the foundation. Who knows when that thing is coming down! Instability and weakness characterize the male who lacks integrity. He can't keep a job. He can't stay married. He can't maintain his reputation. He's unstable.

His foundation is soft, weak, unstable and unsafe. Think about the damage weak men cause to those who depend on him! Even the world recognizes this version of weak manhood as toxic but strong men are the unsung heroes of the world. When a man gets it—everyone wins. But when a man doesn't get it— everyone around him is in danger. His world is always on the brink of crashing down on those who love him the most. Those who have been damaged by his choices to remain an immature boy are left to suffer in the wake of his life.

How many tragic stories do church leaders have to hear before church dollars reflect the value of investing in men? Author and men's leader Robert Lewis appropriately calls a church's failure to strategically value men, "The Big Miss." He's absolutely right. We can fight to stop sex trafficking. We can battle against poverty. We can declare war on alcohol and drugs. These are all noble causes that demand our immediate attention. But when we dive headlong into rectifying these horrible injustices it's vital to realize that we are only putting a Band-Aid on a global problem. Battling these injustices is a means to an end but not an end in itself.

Most of the world's problems have males at the source. When we fix the males, we will eradicate eighty percent of these injustices.

Lastly, buildings and men are built to stay upright. Can you imagine walking up the 296 steps (294 on the other side) in the Leaning Tower of Pisa? The further you climbed, the more it sloped, and the more you would wonder if this was your last day on earth!

We've unpacked why the Tower of Pisa leans. What about a man? What prevents a weak man from standing upright? Better yet, what causes a once-strong man to lean? Let's investigate the relationship between alignment and integrity in the next chapter.

Strengthen Your Grip
Small Group Exercise

Why is integrity foundational for every man? Think about your life. Where are you leaning? How can you rectify this?

In Matthew 7:24-27 Jesus said, "Therefore everyone who hears these words of Mine and acts on them, may be compared to a wise man who built his house on the rock. And the rain fell, and the floods came, and the winds blew and slammed against that house; and yet it did not fall, for it had been founded on the rock.

Everyone who hears these words of Mine and does not act on them, will be like a foolish man who built his house on the sand. The rain fell, and the floods came, and the winds blew and slammed against that house; and it fell—and great was its fall." How are faith and integrity similar? How are they inseparable?

Saint Augustine wrote, "Do you wish to rise? Begin by descending. You plan a tower that will pierce the clouds? Lay first the foundation of humility." Besides humility, what are some other character traits you are working on to strengthen your foundation?

How does any breach of integrity create instability? Share about a time when life became unstable because of an integrity breach on your part.

SLIPPED DISC
The Functional Component of Manhood

"Be more concerned with your character than your reputation."
~John Wooden,
Ten-time National Champion
UCLA basketball coach (1964-1975)

Look straight ahead. Fix your eyes on what lies before you. Mark out a straight
path for your feet; stay on the safe path. Don't get sidetracked; keep your feet
from following evil.
~Proverbs 4:27

"A shortcut usually demands a compromise of integrity. The ironic thing about
these seemingly insignificant compromises is that they both accelerate our
progress and undermine our success. The shortcut allows us to cut down the time
it takes to reach our destination. But the compromise of integrity carves the heart
out of our celebration once we get there."
~Andy Stanley: Visioneering

Functional Workouts?

While working out one morning I felt a strange twinge in my lower back. The pain was minimal but wouldn't go away, radiating down my backside into my foot. It was a pain I'd never experienced before. Very few positions offered relief. The pain got stronger, coming to a climax while doing dead lifts at the gym.

I know what you're thinking, "You should have rested longer idiot." Hindsight is 20/20. Back to the story.

I rounded my back on my last rep of 225 pounds (no lecture please) and that was all it took. I felt something slip in my lower back and intense nerve pain shot through my right glute, down my hamstring, around the calf, and into my foot.

. . .

Within a few weeks I couldn't feel my outside three toes. My doctor offered no natural solution. The chiropractor worked diligently to bring healing, but I still couldn't find relief. I can't do the pain justice by explaining it. I couldn't sit without pain. I couldn't stand for more than a few minutes. Bending over to tie my shoes literally brought tears to my eyes. I eventually bought slip-ons. Thank God for Romeos by Georgia Boots! The pain was indescribable and virtually inescapable.

I was incapacitated for almost two years until I hesitantly decided to have back surgery after the discovery that I had slipped—herniated—the disc between my L5 and S1 vertebrae.

Since then the pain has faded (for the most part), feeling has returned to my foot (thankfully), and I am back at full capacity (mostly). However, today I live and think differently. I'm more cautious. I'm smart when injured and rest until healed (usually). I avoid twisting whenever picking something up. I think of a small silver-dollar-sized-disc moving just a fraction of an inch, those two years of indescribable suffering, and never want to repeat them.

That gel disc barely slipped *out of alignment* and changed my life and the lives of those who loved me the most, who were compelled to care for me. I lost energy. I was immobilized. My emotional tank was empty. I functioned at less than full capacity, and although I wanted to engage with my family I had no bandwidth to function at my previous level. I was instantly transformed from a strong man to a weaker one. A man who provided for others needed others to provide for him. A powerful man, in many ways became impotent, weak, and pathetic.

This story is an illustration and warning that when our integrity is out of alignment, even if it's just a fraction, our life begins to veer off course. In the short run it appears trivial and indiscriminate, but over time it's debilitating.

That notorious disc didn't suddenly shift. It happened slowly, on at least three occasions. The injury happened in March. I ignored it because I'm a "strong" man. By May it was getting bothersome. By June I was officially injured. But by September I was crippled. At that point in September, all effort, energy, and focus went to recovering from an injury that could have been avoided had I only caught the signs early and taken the necessary steps to prevent further damage.

Outwardly I looked the same but could not function to my normal capacity because (combined with stupidity) an indiscriminate gel disc moved ever so slightly. Those two years taught me that function is better—by far—than form.

Function over Form

Integrity is the functional component of manhood because it enables a man to live among his circle with the highest reputation, whether at his job, in his home, or among his community. Listen to what God spoke about Job's integrity: *"Have you considered My servant Job? For there is no one like him on the earth, a blameless and **upright** man fearing God and turning away from evil. And he still holds fast his integrity, although you incited Me against him to ruin him without cause" (Job 2:3 NASB).*

Let's go back to my back injury for a second. I was literally unable to function in an upright position for extended periods of time. The pain was too great. I had to lie flat whenever possible.

Job's integrity, however, allowed him to function "upright" and in full view of his world. It allowed Job to function as the best version of himself, unlike so many today who duck and hide behind their secret lives. Did you know that the human species is the only mammal, besides Sasquatch of course, that walks completely upright with his reproductive organs exposed? God designed humans to literally walk in full view of the world. He created us in His image to walk upright and on full display for the world to see the glory of God.

But what happened? Adam and Eve broke God's covenant? Without wading too far into the weeds, let's look at Genesis 3:6-7:

> When the woman saw that the tree was good for food, and that it
> was a delight to the eyes, and that the tree was desirable to
> make one wise, she took from its fruit and ate; and she gave
> also to her husband with her, and he ate. Then the eyes of both
> of them were opened, and they knew that they were naked;
> and they sewed fig leaves together and made themselves loin
> coverings (NASB).

Unlike Job, Adam's lack of integrity literally left him hunched over covering his shame with fig leaves! Can you imagine Adam bent over, hands covering his private parts from the view of his own wife! This is what happens when a man has a breach of integrity. He's left bent over covering his shame, unable to stand upright in full view of the world. We must be diligent to protect our integrity in all compartments of life: marriage, family, church, work, hobbies, and friendships. Integrity must bleed into every part of life to maintain an upright status.

Unlike our wonderful women counterparts, men tend to separate their thoughts, roles, and actions. Women tend to connect them. In other words, men generally compartmentalize how they process information and life. We have the unique ability to give complete focus to one thing at a time. We're the masters of focus and our compartments rarely overlap. We might be doing great in one area of character because of intense focus and neglect other critical issues.

What we fail to realize—women understand this better—is that if any compartment is incomplete, broken, or missing, the whole of integrity is affected. If one aspect of character is missing, we are incomplete and lack integrity. If I'm in that state, both I, and those who depend on me are in danger.

Think of a man you once respected but at some point, had something similar happen that took him out of the game. He was publicly shamed, embarrassed, and humiliated because of his poor choices. At first you were shocked but looking back you saw the warning signs. It was barely visible at first. Looking back however, you saw the signs—one small compromise, then another, slightly larger, then another. Until one day it all came crashing down. Today he walks with a moral limp, slightly hunched over, trying to gather the courage to walk fully upright once more. He is an eggshell of the man he once was, because he allowed compromise to run its tragic course.

We've all been at such points of compromise. Some catch it early and get back on track while others, for whatever reason, ignore the signs as their integrity slips further and further. Compromising our integrity is progressive. Fix it before it destroys you.

One reason that men fail to fix a breach of integrity is their difficulty in combining the various traits. For example, I can be a strong man of character except for, let's say, a small pornography problem. If I look at porn once a month but refuse to confess and repent of it, I'm in danger. This one area, this one breach, has the damaging potential to cause great shame, humiliation, and embarrassment not only to me, but to those who love me the most. I can be "upright" in *most areas* of my life but if I'm hunched over by sin in just one, my integrity is lacking. Every other area of my life might be in order, but this single breach can ruin my life if not dealt with in a Biblical manner. That's why it's so important to have trusted men who have our backs and are willing to call us out.

Integrity is the **functional component of manhood.** Without it a man can't function as the best version of himself. He can't function at full capacity. Integrity is the backbone of manhood just as a man is the backbone of his family. When a man gets it—everyone wins. Conversely, when a man fails to get it—everyone loses.

When you think of integrity as functional, think of the word "upright" that was used to describe Job in our chapter introduction. *Upright* describes my ability to maneuver with a healed back. You've seen the commercial of the man hunched over holding his lower back. Imagine that man when you consider integrity as the functional component of manhood.

Hindsight Is 20/20

Let's review with the four things I learned about integrity from my back injury.

Uno, my **posture** was highly affected. I was forced to focus on how I stood and moved to ensure the least amount of pain. The more I hunched over the worse it hurt. The only comfortable position was lying flat on my back without engaging the lower back muscles. I avoided being seen in public because that meant standing, walking, or sitting upright (there's that word again). The worst position was sitting down with my right leg extended. Like when driving a car!

Because speaking is a large part of my ministry, getting to events took creativity. When flying to a speaking event in Colorado I actually had to travel in the luggage compartment with the pets and rest on a cot I brought from home! I'm just kidding. It wasn't *that* bad! I did have to recruit friends and family to drive me to speaking events while I laid down in the back of my truck. Now, that is true! A solo speaking engagement trip to Washington was especially memorable!

Figuratively, posture is affected by the presence—or absence—of my integrity. Integrity allows me to live upright and in full view of others without fear, hesitation, or doubt. It's to live in full confidence that the world can experience the best version of me—that the public and private me are the same man!

Dos, my **potential** is limited. With my back I couldn't even bend over to tie my shoes. I wore flip-flops and slip-on boots for almost everything during those two years. It hurt to walk. I couldn't run, hike, or lift weights. It took great effort to stand, sit in a chair, or drive a car. I could only work about twenty hours a week because of the pain. Looking back, maybe I should've taken pain medication, but I'd much rather learn to deal with the pain than be numbed by and dependent upon any pain medication.

Tres, I learned what worsened the pain and how to **prevent** it. I became an expert on nerve pain prevention, and developed habits to lessen it. I stopped twisting my torso altogether. I bend over with my back straight when I pick up any object. When my back starts to hurt, I stop and rest it instead of trying to push through.

When we loosen our grip on integrity and slip into old behaviors, pain is knocking at the door. We must realize that any breach in integrity leads to pain of some kind. The fruit of an integrity breach is pain. Sow compromise and reap pain. It's not Karma. It's just simple.

Quatro, before the injury I moved freely without thought. I was free. I was mobile. I took advantage of my freedom without a second thought, but no more. Post injury, I'm more **proactive** than ever. I'm thoughtful of my back. I'm fully aware of what my back is saying. I'm totally engaged. Every workout, every upper body movement, and every leisure activity is now considered and weighed on the basis of my back. I'm not passive regarding my back. I'm engaged. I'm proactive.

Integrity must be handled in the same manner. Consider *all compartments* in your life. Be engaged. Be accountable for your integrity with people you trust. Don't be neutral. Do not sit idly by but shift your integrity into high gear.

Strengthen Your Grip
Small Group Exercise

John Wooden, ten-time National Champion basketball coach for UCLA from 1964-1975, said, "Be more concerned with your character than your reputation." What does this mean? How are character and integrity similar? Different?

Proverbs 4:27 warns us to: "Look straight ahead. Fix your eyes on what lies before you. Mark out a straight path for your feet; stay on the safe path. Don't get sidetracked; keep your feet from following evil." In what ways does this proverb speak to integrity?

John F. Kennedy said. "A rising tide causes all ships to lift." How do you see something similar with men of integrity? What does your inner circle of friends say about your integrity?

Integrity is the functional component of manhood. Without it a man can't function as the best version of himself. He can't function at full capacity. Integrity is the backbone of manhood just as a man is the backbone of his family. How have you seen this reality in your life? Where have you been hindered by personal failure?

FRONT END ALIGNMENT
The Fight for Integrity

"I came to get a front end alignment, and instead got a total life overhaul."
~David, "Front End Alignment" Seminar Attendee
Terre Haute, Indiana

The highway of the upright avoids evil; those who guard their ways preserve
their lives.
~Proverbs 16:17

"We're only given one life to live, but if we do it right; once is enough."
~Joe "The Brown Bomber" Louis

The Seminar

So far, we've explained how integrity is different from character. We've argued that a man lacking integrity is missing the key to unlocking his manhood potential. We've boldly explained that integrity is the first step in becoming a strong man—without it a male remains just a male regardless of his manly appearance, age, success, anatomy, or legal status.

We've also discussed that integrity is foundational to the making and sustaining of a man. It's not only foundational but also functional. How a man interacts with integrity, or the lack thereof, directly affects how he interacts with, and is seen by, those around him.

It's critical to note before moving on that integrity is *not* one of the five essential components of the man seeking his strongest version— protecting integrity is. Protecting integrity as in the progressive tense of the verb *to protect*. It means constantly battling for your integrity with every decision made, every day of your life.

Men don't earn integrity without a fight, just as fish don't drift upstream. Living things stand strong, move freely, and will swim against the current when called. Dead things drift. When we stop protecting integrity, like a post-spawn salmon, we drift downstream to a stagnant pool of death, decay, and decomposition.

. . .

This chapter is written with emotion. After watching the devastating effects of dozens of men I care about crash and burn, protecting integrity must remain at the top of the list. I've witnessed strong men fall because, weakened, they surrendered to the currents of society ending in devastating failures. Witnessing the wake of those choices crash into these men we commissioned to protect is heartbreaking.

Be forewarned. It's a slow fade. The signs of drift start with small choices but compound over time to become disastrous. As I travel the country speaking to men my **Front-End Alignment** seminar has become a signature message. I'll never forget the email I received from a man in Indiana soon after hearing my message. He wrote, *"I came to get a 'Front End Alignment', but instead got a total life overhaul."*

Incredibly, he showed up one year later in a different state to hear the same message, this time bringing his two sons and his pastor! I've watched numerous pastors over the years—dozens—serve for decades only to leave town with their tail between their legs because they couldn't keep something else between their legs under control. Sadly, since age twenty-two, not one of my senior pastors retired as a pastor. Not one. Either by moral failure or leaving to pursue another career (not necessarily an integrity problem), each eventually left the ministry. Reflecting on many of these once strong men and their drift, I want to pass on several insights that will change your life, if you're willing to receive them.

First, what do I mean by front end alignment?

The man in *alignment* is when the man you publicly claim to be matches the private man you actually are. When your public and private life is synonymous, you're a man in alignment—a man of integrity. Let's crank it up a notch. When your thoughts match your words *and* actions, you're in alignment. Let's not get too dogmatic here. We're all broken on some level and can't fully measure up to this standard, but aren't you glad we have an example to follow in Jesus; *"For we do not have a high priest who cannot sympathize with our weaknesses, but One who has been tempted in all things as we are, yet without sin" (Hebrews 4:15b).*

If your actions don't match your beliefs, words and thoughts, you're a man that is *out of* alignment. Let me restate from our previous chapter. If just *one of your character traits* is out of order, then you're lacking in integrity. Integrity is being complete, whole, and unbroken in every character trait. If one area of your character is infected, then you've been compromised.

Life is hard. It's draining. Its propensity is to pull us off course into oncoming traffic. When a man lets go of the wheel, he won't stay on course but will drift away from center. Those we love, those sleeping unaware in the back seat, depend on us to stay focused, alert, and with our hands on the wheel at all times.

When our three sons were infants and toddlers, we'd take our annual road trip from our California home to Grandma Haley's in Eagle, Idaho. We'd be in such a rush to vacate that I'd pack the night before and go from my office seat to the car seat, and drive through the night! Those trips weren't possible if not for Shanna riding shotgun and keeping me awake. The most dangerous times were when, exhausted, she'd drift to sleep in the early morning hours.

The fallen men I've observed had no **navigator.** No one was riding shotgun. No one—whether by choice or not (I don't know)—had their back. They were isolated. They were closed. They had no *functioning* accountability guy or group. Whether it was because of their own pride, gutless friends, or refusal to confess their secrets, I don't know. But they veered off course without notice from those closest to them and ultimately crashed and burned.

Strong men don't travel alone. Like the African proverb, "If you want to go fast, go alone; but if you want to go far, go together." Strong men have a trusted band of brothers who have the guts to call us out on our *skubala* (Greek for human excrement). Weak men do not.

If you have men like this in your life, thank God for them! If not, find a man, or group of men, and trust them! You will be strengthened because of them. In his wisdom, Jesus compared life to a road, *"Enter through the narrow gate. For wide is the gate and broad is the road that leads to destruction, and many enter through it. But small is the gate and narrow the road that leads to life, and only a few find it" (Matthew 7:13-14).* The trail Jesus blazed is a narrow one. Ironically it can't be traveled alone. Ironically, according to Jesus the road to destruction is wide, broad, and is often traveled alone. In the rest of this chapter we'll travel to the end of the narrow road of life.

Keep reading, slowly. Your integrity, and your life depend on it.

Misaligned Tire

Imagine a worn-out tire. Standing over it you observe that the treads have worn unevenly. One side is exposed to the steel walls while the other is still covered with tread—a sure sign of being out of alignment. This tire would have been usable for thousands of additional miles if it hadn't worn unevenly. But here it is in the dumpster, replaced **before its time.**

At some point the wheel it was mounted on got knocked out of alignment and never realigned. How it happened, we'll never know. But once the wheel was knocked out of alignment it was **pulled in the wrong direction.** Most of you know exactly what an out of aligned tire feels like. Correcting the course of the misaligned wheels requires a little pressure on the steering wheel to keep the car driving straight, creating unwanted wear on an otherwise good tire. Letting go of the steering wheel we see the problem as the car veers instantly off course.

Similarly, an out of alignment man is also pulled off course. He is weaker and wears out sooner than a stronger man. He veers if pressure isn't constantly applied. He complains that his wife "nags" at him. His boss becomes a "jerk". His pastor is suddenly "judgmental". Added pressures from those who care about him become burdensome, but without them he will crash.

If not realigned the tire will wear out sooner than it was designed to. When a man is out of alignment, he maintains his public persona, but it soon becomes a web of lies, as he spins his wheels in an attempt to hide his private life from his public image.

This comes at a cost. The burden of sin, pressure to appear in alignment, and the web of lies take time and energy—lots of it. Eventually, these wear him down. And he weakens. He loses stamina and wears out sooner than he would have if he were in alignment.

Eventually he is exposed, hopefully before he's too far off course. Hopefully he still has some tread left once he's realigned, because once the steel tread is exposed a blowout is inevitable. If caught early, it can be dealt with before consequences are disastrous and collateral damage is monumental.

It doesn't have to be the case, but without corrective measures, a wheel that is out of alignment is the beginning of the end for a tire—and a man—that once had great strength.

Sometimes the male involved is never exposed. I realize this. I'm not that naïve. He lives out his secret life as an underdeveloped male until the day he dies. His weakness is clearly visible, but it's ignored or adopted as the norm. Some former friends avoid him. He becomes increasingly isolated and alone. He lives an underachiever's life. He bathes himself in sin and mediocrity. Those who should be receiving benefit from him end up neglected, abused, and wounded. He lives in the stands of anonymity, never fully entering the arena where the strong men reside.

Is that the type of man you want to be?

Like the misaligned wheel, the misaligned man **gets rattled** more easily than before. He's constantly on guard, fighting to protect the illusion that he's more than he actually is. He defends his actions like the charlatan he is. It's tough to manage two lives—secret and public—the web of lies gets difficult for even him to discern. When caught in one of his lies he'll resort to anger or another heightened emotion to cover his tracks. If he would only commit to the pursuit of integrity his life would become so much smoother and simpler.

Misaligned wheels ride rougher than those in alignment. The misaligned man is in for a **rough** ride. Even if never exposed, he won't become the best version of himself. I'm not a mechanic, but I know when something is off. I know when my truck has a problem even if I can't identify what it is. It's similar to the misaligned man. His marriage will be lacking, and he'll wonder why. Relationships with his children will be strained. His career will suffer. People won't be able to put a finger on it. They'll just know something is off.

Tragically, the misaligned man, like the tire, is often **replaced before his time.** The misalignment is never dealt with, the tread wears unevenly, steel is exposed, there's a massive blowout, sometimes resulting in a crash. I've dealt with many men who have been exposed. *It ain't pretty.* For example, if the marriage survives an adulterous blowout—that's a big "if"—experts say it takes *at least* three to five years for the betrayed spouse to trust the betrayer again.

Bumps in the Road

Like a wheel, several things can knock a man out of alignment. Let's look at six alignment adjusters, but I admit there may be more.

A man is knocked out of alignment when he hits an **unforeseen bump** in the road of life—the loss of a job, a serious illness or injury, or unexpected tragedy, to list a few. Life is full of unforeseen obstacles. Be ready. Look ahead. There's an ominous pothole down the road somewhere. I guarantee it. If we aren't prepared it'll knock us out of alignment.

Secret habits cause more damage than pleasure. Scott Hagan, President of North Central University says, "Whatever you can't talk about, **owns you.**" I couldn't agree more. Romans 2:16 warns, "On the day...God will judge the secrets of men through Christ Jesus." Missionary and martyr, Jim Elliot once said, "When it comes time to die, make sure all you got to do is die." I beg you, confess any secret habits that will ruin you if they become exposed, such as pornography, adultery, gluttony (obesity is result of sin), gambling, alcohol, or drug abuse. Commit to a life in alignment, a life of integrity.

Allowing the **wrong people** in your inner circle will definitely change how you live. *The Association Principle* simply stated is, "Birds of a feather flock together. Like begets like. Water seeks its own level. You are the average of the top five people you spend the most time with." Choose your inner circle wisely, friend. Over time it will define you. I love what President John F. Kennedy once said, "A rising tide causes all ships to lift." Similarly, low tide has the same effect.

Pursuing the **wrong trophies.** Don't believe the lie that your portfolio defines your worth. What a crock! Jesus had no home. In Matthew 8:20 Jesus reminds, *"The foxes have holes and the birds of the air have nests, but the Son of Man has nowhere to lay His head."* He was supported financially, in part, by a group of women. He was never given accolades in Scripture for his vocational skills or worldly wealth. Yet he stands in eternity as the ultimate man and Savior of all. The only trophy worth pursuing is the Creator of the Universe. We must pursue things in the correct order. When we pursue God before all else, we become our best version.

A man can be knocked out of alignment if he is **wounded.** The Church is notorious for applauding those who over serve. Spiritual leaders will applaud a person's busy lifestyle until they burn out, become wounded, and loathe the organized church. If you're a man in the Stress Bubble of life—you are married and raising children—be very selective about what you say "Yes" to. Trust me. No human or organization is more important than your wife and your children (in that order). I love my local church. It's where I worship, give, serve, and attend. I'm fully aware of its desperate need for volunteers, and the Church's inadvertent propensity to violate people in the name of Jesus through overuse and under-rest. Be warned.

We are misaligned when, for whatever reason, we are **disengaged** from those we're called to love. I was in the Stress Bubble for more than two decades! Being fully engaged "in the Bubble" is the toughest thing I've ever done. But, with God's help, we did it. You can too. Centuries of strong men have gone before us.

I want to confess something: upon the writing of this book, I'm tired, my energy is diminished, and quite frankly, I'm a little worn out. The Stress Bubble is quite literally a stress bubble. I've been a good husband and father. I still am. But it's tough. Stay engaged with those you love and are called to lead. You're in this for the long haul. *Your heritage depends on what you do with the rest of your time in the Stress Bubble.* Be wise with your priorities, time, and relationships. Pace yourself to finish strong. So many have finished wrong. Don't be that guy.

Stay in alignment. Have a band of brothers keep you in check so that the man you are in public and the man you are in private are the same man. Potholes, rocks, and other debris threatening to knock you out of alignment mark the road of life. Be aware.

Protecting Integrity is a daily battle. Traveling down the road of life without getting knocked out of alignment is a struggle for sure. Yes! It's a battle. No, it's war but one you will win.

Strengthen Your Grip
Small Group Exercise

At the beginning of this chapter Jim wrote, "It's critical to note before moving on that integrity is *not* one of the five essential components of the man seeking his strongest version—protecting integrity is." Why is this so important to understand?

What did Solomon mean in Proverbs 16:17 when he wrote, "The highway of the upright avoids evil; those who guard their ways preserve their lives?"

What does it mean to be a man in alignment? Conversely, how do you know when you are not in alignment? Where do you need a life alignment?

Joe "The Brown Bomber" Louis said, "We're only given one life to live, but if we do it right, once is enough." How do his words encourage you to realign yourself when things get out of whack?

PART II

THE CLIMB: FIGHTING APATHY

ROAD LESS TRAVELED
The Narrow Winding Road

"Two roads diverged in a yellow wood, and sorry I could not travel both And be one traveler, long I stood and looked down one as far as I could To where it bent in the undergrowth; Then took the other, as just as fair, and having perhaps the better claim, Because it was grassy and wanted wear; though as for that the passing there Had worn them really about the same, And both that morning equally lay in leaves no step had trodden black. Oh, I kept the first for another day! Yet knowing how way leads on to way, I doubted if I should ever come back. I shall be telling this with a sigh somewhere ages and ages hence: Two roads diverged in a wood, and I—I took the one less traveled by, And that has made all the difference."
~Robert Frost
Poem: The Road Not Taken

Enter through the narrow gate. For wide is the gate and broad is the road that leads to destruction, and many enter through it. But small is the gate and narrow the road that leads to life, and only a few find it.
~Matthew 7:13-14

"Our greatest danger is letting the urgent things crowd out the important. We live in constant tension between the urgent and the important."
~Charles Hummel

Gravity

Last summer a close friend invited some of us men out to his home in Hawaii for a "mancation". Our plan was to fish, mountain bike, rest, and repeat. It was an epic time filled with memory making experiences with great friends. But the mountain bike rides nearly broke me, physically, and mentally. The giant seven to twelve mile climbs stole something from me that took over a year to recover. Prior to the trip, my mountain biking experience was to climb the mountain **first** and reap the rewards of the downhill thrill last. In other words, each ride, no matter how difficult the climb, was remembered by the last memory—a hair-raising rush of the downhill experience.

Since my friend lives near the top of the island every ride **began** with an epic downhill and ended with a grinding climb of no less than 2500 feet of vertical gain in mid-80-degree heat! At 250 pounds you can only imagine what that does to a man. I was reminded, the hard way that added weight hinders on climbs—in a big way. Every pound matters when fighting gravity.

To stop pedaling meant falling off the bike because the only power up was in your burning quads. A failure to overcome the mountain's uphill grade meant zero elevation gain. So, grinding away, I climbed one pedal stroke after another, one vertical foot at a time, until reaching the top.

What was the emotion concluding each ride? It wasn't the thrill of adrenaline as I raced my lighter buddies down the mountain. It was pain and suffering. To this day the only thing able to talk me out of a ride is the grinding climb.

The second of the five essentials that strong men leverage is **fighting apathy.** It's like fighting gravity in a grueling climb up a mountain. It's a climb that fewer men are willing to take. It's much easier to jump off, slack off, and back off, than to grind it out on the way to the top.

Too many males defer their role as a man to others. Sadly, our society doesn't applaud a man. It presses in against him. It tells him that the best way to be a man is to become a woman, or worse yet, to be gender neutral. It's easy to take a knee, take a seat, and take it easy. But men don't take shortcuts. They don't coast. They commit to the climb.

Straight and Narrow Road?

In this section of *Strong Men Dangerous Times,* you'll learn that the greatest battle men fight isn't against the damaging effects of lust, adultery, or pornography. It's not the horrific injustice of the sex trade and sex trafficking. It's not greed, materialism, or financial indebtedness. It's not pride, politics, or prejudice. It's the root cause of all of the above—**apathy.**

That's right. Fighting apathy is the greatest battle of our time. Stu Weber rightly called this generation the "era of the soft male." By "soft" he referred to adult males that are weak, impotent, and apathetic—not caring—towards other people, deferring their responsibilities for the well-being of others. A synonym of apathy is indifference. Modern males have shrugged their shoulders and deferred the honor of carrying the baton to whoever else is willing.

In *Section Two* we ended our discussion on *Protecting Integrity* with the warning that protecting integrity is a daily battle. It's a battle because the propensity of human nature is to get out of alignment. But protecting integrity isn't the greatest battle. *The great war against all of the forces against our best version finds its most crucial battle right here: fighting apathy.*

As I travel the country speaking to men, I often get deer-in-the-headlight-stares when I introduce *fighting apathy* as one of the five essentials of manhood. When a man lets go of the wheel he will naturally drift into apathy, which manifests itself in dangerous forms. It's in our nature to drift. Men who drift into apathy will also drift into all kinds of male muck and mire. Fight life's tendencies to pull you off course. Don't drift!

The Right Road

This chapter is the most practical in this book. Picture life as a **narrow, rough, and winding road**, then navigate it accurately, and you'll experience what Jesus called, *"Life to its fullest" (John 10:10b)*.

There are many road options but only one right road. Unlike the ancient phrase, all roads lead to Rome, all roads **do not** lead to being a man. Jesus said, *"I am the way, and the truth, and the life; no one comes to the Father but through Me" (John 14:6)*. The road less traveled is treacherous. It has dangerous twists and turns. It has potholes, dips, and potentially deadly debris.

You can travel on whatever road you want. It's your choice. Everyone is entitled to choose his destiny. You'll choose yours. I encourage you to transcend your personal opinions and do some objective research. I think you'll discover that **Jesus** is who he says he is, did what he said he would, and is waiting for us at the end—for those who are on the right road. In spite of life's blind corners, treacherous conditions, and reckless drivers, He is the only one with a promise waiting for us at the end.

See the end of the road now. It may be tough. Life has many corners. Sometimes it's difficult to see what's around the next bend. Life isn't as cut and dry as we'd like to make it. Brothers, Jesus knows what it is to walk a tough and bloody road! And when we have a riveting vision of Jesus waiting at our road's end, we'll keep grinding through whatever life throws at us.

,

Black and White World

Unlike what I thought in my first three decades, life isn't a straight and narrow road. I wish it were that simple. The **black and white world** of my twenties was dogmatic, legalistic, and zealous. But it was clean. It was crystal clear. It was simple. People were this, or that. God was this, not that. Life was like this, but if you lived it wrong, it was like that. Shanna and I joke that the 1990's were my "legalistic" decade, but I prefer to call them my "zealous" years. Then something traumatic happened.

I grew up.

I experienced the messiness of life while working at a church on California's Central Coast. Churches are a wonderful, yet painful conduit to walk with people through their pain. In between the beach communities of Los Osos and Morro Bay—the place where fog was invented—I experienced life's gray moments of ministry through the local church. There I learned that life wasn't simple but complex. It wasn't black or white but something in between. It wasn't smooth, straight, or simple, but rough and winding. God didn't fit into my box. Does He ever? I saw the innocent die. I witnessed human suffering. I felt the pain of divorce. I held the hands of good people dying. It shook my black and white world to the core.

We don't have all the answers. Anyone who claims to is a liar. We have more questions—way more. Life is tenuous. There's a paradox to life that all must accept as we pursue God. In our weakness God gives strength. When we die, then we live. When we surrender, then we receive. When we're weak, then we're strong. My body is diminishing but my spirit is being renewed. When I mourn, then I find comfort. My present pain is a future blessing.

Some tensions lead us closer to God. Others pull us away. In the midst of this paradoxical world we must discern between the truth and the lie. We fight against those things that threaten to pull us off course.

There's another tension that strong men discover as they enter the Stress Bubble of marriage, family, and a career. Life in the "Bubble" is characterized by tremendous pressure. Brian Doyle, founder of the Iron Sharpens Iron Men's Conferences, recently shared on the Men in the Arena Podcast that, "Men are made for pressure."

I couldn't agree more.

. . .

Men are forged under pressure and fire. Our resilience comes with the ability to resist the pressures threatening to push us off the mountain of manhood. If we fail to resist life's pressures, they'll wear us down.

If you're a guy who lifts weights or does manual labor, you've probably noticed something. Over time your hands form calluses from the constant friction demanded of them. Initially you had blisters, but over time your hands passively adapted to the constant friction; thus, a callus formed. A callus is a dead, nerveless, thickening of skin resulting from friction.

Calluses on the hands are meant to protect us from pain, but when the heart becomes calloused; a man loses feeling for things that should be highly emotive. When he fails to resist lies, he becomes apathetic, indifferent, and passive. He disengages from his marriage, ignores his children, and becomes a consumer rather than a contributor. Fighting apathy is the man that resists the forces threatening to deaden his spirit.

End of the Road

Earlier I asked you to see the end of the road: to have a vision for your life. Henry Cloud in his book, *Nine Things You Simply Must Do,* admonishes readers to "Play the movie (of your life)." Steven Covey in his classic work, *The Seven Habits of Highly Effective People,* offered similar advice: "See the end at the beginning."

What do you want written as the **epitaph** on your grave marker? What short sentence will define your life?

Narrow your 80+ years of life down to a sentence. Can you pull it off? Most of us will be remembered by a few people for a handful of meaningful things we did in those 80 years. At every memorial service I've attended, or officiated, there's usually a theme (two at most) describing the life of the deceased. What will yours be? Don't turn this page until you've scribbled your one sentence epitaph on the margin.

- I'm waiting.
- Go on, write your epitaph to the right of this.
- You have plenty of space now.
- No excuses. Okay, let's move on!

Several years ago, I did something life changing. I went beyond a one sentence epitaph and wrote my eulogy. I've read it every year since. No kidding. Write the newspaper column that describes your life posthumously. What were your accomplishments and fond memories of loved ones? Someday someone will write this. It may as well be you. You're dying. So am I. We're all dying one day at a time. Death is imminent. There's something profound about a visionary trip to the end of your life and in that vision to look back towards where you are now.

You've scribbled your epitaph in the margin—now write your **eulogy** in the back of this book. It will change your life like it changed mine.

Here's some advice to help you. One, do it now. Stop reading after this chapter and write your epitaph on the back of this book. Two, write from a family member's point of view—your wife, a child, or a close friend. Three, limit your eulogy to under 1000 words. Four, keep it realistic. This isn't the news. This is truth. Imagine how your choices today will affect tomorrow. Your choices today and the values you live by, compounded over time, equal your life. Five, review it no less than once a year to track your progress.

Don't blow this off thinking, "That's a great idea! I'll do it later." Stop reading. Turn to the back page and reflect on your life so far, choices you've made, and dreams for your future.

Get to work.

Strengthen Your Grip
Small Group Exercise

Of the five essentials, Jim calls fighting apathy the "grind of life." Why does he believe fighting apathy is the "greatest battle of our time?"

In Matthew 7:13-14 Jesus said, "Enter through the narrow gate. For wide is the gate and broad is the road that leads to destruction, and many enter through it. But small is the gate and narrow the road that leads to life, and only a few find it." How is fighting apathy connected to strong men and a dynamic faith?

Men are forged under pressure and fire. Our resilience comes with the ability to resist the pressures threatening to push us off the mountain of manhood. If we fail to resist life's pressures, they'll wear us down. What are you being pressed hard for right now? Who has your back? How do they push you?

Charles Hummel said, "Our greatest danger is letting the urgent things crowd out the important. We live in constant tension between the urgent and the important." What important things are often neglected because of your focus on the urgent? How has your neglect jeopardized the deep feelings you should have towards these people and things?

CUTTING AWAY CALLUSES
A Man's Greatest Battle

*"To see the world, things dangerous to come to, to see behind walls, draw closer,
to find each other, and to feel. That is the purpose of life."*
~Movie, The Secret Life of Walter Mitty

*"Though seeing, they do not see; though hearing, they do not hear or
understand. In them is fulfilled the prophecy of Isaiah: 'You will be ever hearing
but never understanding; you will be ever seeing but never perceiving. For this
people's heart has become calloused; they hardly hear with their ears, and they
have closed their eyes. Otherwise they might see with their eyes, hear with their
ears, understand with their hearts and turn, and I would heal them.'"*
~Matthew 13:13-15

*"They say that I can move the mountains and send them crashing to the sea.
They say that I can walk on water if I would follow and believe with faith like a
child. They say that love can heal the broken. They say that hope can make you
see. They say that faith can find a Savior. If you would follow and believe with
faith like a child."*
~Jars of Clay
Song, "Like a Child"

Wikipedia describes apathy as, "A state of indifference, or the suppression of emotions such as concern, excitement, motivation and passion. An apathetic individual has an absence of interest in or concern about emotional, social, spiritual, philosophical and/or physical life."

The word **apathy** originates from the ancient Greek word **apathēs**—without feeling. The word was never used before 1594, which is why there is no mention of it in the Bible. You may be wondering, "Then why use it in defining one of the five aspects of manhood?"

You mean, besides it being the greatest battle a man will ever fight?

The word may not be found in Scripture but it was the cause of Adam's sin—the fall of man—in Genesis 3. It's the reason Jesus searched for, found, and rebuked the paralytic healed at the pool of Bethesda (John 5:14). It's what our

Lord defeated in the Garden of Gethsemane the night before his death (Matthew 26:36-46). And, tragically, it's the downfall of contemporary males around the world.

Callus or Callous?

A synonym of apathy in Scripture is callousness. Here's a fun English lesson I learned when researching this book. The physical hardening of my hands from manual labor is called a callus. It's a **physical** sign of unrestrained friction over time. Construction workers are all too familiar with calluses. I get calluses from lifting weights or doing yard work without wearing gloves. Calluses protect the hands and feet from blistering. There are no nerve endings in calluses so you can cut, rip, or grind them off without feeling pain.

However, if the hardening is not physical but **figurative**—say over my heart —I become callous. When a human heart becomes calloused it becomes indifferent and insensitive to the things a healthy heart would care about deeply.

You'll see the spelling changes throughout this book so it's fun to know why.

Like a Glove

Gloves are worn to protect the hands from blisters. Blisters are the result of constant friction. Gloves prevent friction by creating a protective layer between the hands and the tool. Gloves maintain the sensitivity in the hands by preventing the friction the tool (say a hammer) would otherwise create. Without gloves the friction between the worker's tool and hands form a blister over time. To protect ungloved hands, blisters eventually evolve into **calluses**. Thus, the hands eventually became **calloused** (note the spelling change)—hard, tough, and unfeeling. It still confuses me at times.

Calluses are the body's way of protecting itself against constant exposure to the elements and potential infection when a blister opens up. For the body's sake, a callus is a good thing.

But for the heart's sake, calluses formed over time have tragic consequences. You should resist any thing, event, or person that threatens to harden your heart.

The problem, however, is that a man's life is characterized by tension. Strong men lean into this pressure, where weaker men avoid it like the plague. Strong men place themselves in high pressure situations to test their strength, where weaker men retreat into their comfort zones. Strong men use powerful legs to jump into the arena while weaker males sit with their figurative stick legs in the anonymous bleachers. Life's many responsibilities wear a man down if he isn't consciously resisting the pressure. But—catch this—it's resistance that strengthens. Comfort weakens.

Resistance results in strength.

Comfort's byproduct is weakness.

Frederick Douglass rightly said, "It is easier to build strong children than to repair broken men." Declare war on apathy. Fight against it for the sake of your heart and those who have it. Weaker men defer leadership to stronger men as they veer into the apathetic lifestyle, which is really just pathetic with a vowel. They always have and always will.

Life has a way of grinding on a man. Life wears a man down over time. **Fighting apathy** is a daily battle and takes constant work. Don't let life rob you of your heart, passion, and the causes you care deeply about.

Blindfolds and Ear Plugs

Included at the top of this chapter are the words of the ultimate man, Jesus, in Matthew 13:15, *"For this people's heart has become calloused; they **hardly** hear with their ears, and they have **closed** their eyes. Otherwise they might see with their eyes, hear with their ears, understand with their hearts and turn, and I would heal them."*

This is a unique passage of Scripture. It's used three times in three different sections of the Bible: Old Testament (Isaiah 6:8-10), Gospels (Matthew 13:13-15), and the birth of the Church (Acts 28:17-30).

People die every year in rural Oregon where we live while traveling the country roads of the Willamette Valley. Why? Country roads often have no shoulder—no margin for error. If a vehicle veers even three feet off course the next stop is a drainage ditch, injury, and possible death. It's tough to correct once you've drifted off the road even a few inches. When traveling down life's rough, winding, and narrow road, prevention is the best medicine—stay **on the road.**

The amazing passage in scripture offers the two reasons why a heart becomes calloused—not three, not one, just two.

First, a heart can become calloused to the point that it "hardly hear(s)". For example, my hearing has diminished over the years because of *habitual neglect.*

Remember that phrase. I've experienced hearing loss over my lifetime because growing up I never wore hearing protective gear while shooting. Initially, my hearing loss was virtually indiscernible, but over time it means my wife is yelling that I need hearing aids. Huh? What did you say, Honey?

Translation: the **loss of hearing is habitual.** "Hardly hearing" happened after years of unprotected abuse from those deafening elements. Bottom line: my hearing loss is a direct result of habitual neglect. Similarly, the desensitizing voices of culture add calloused layer upon layer over the human heart, which slowly erodes our ability to hear God's voice and feel for the people and causes that matter most. Spiritually speaking, the more I choose my subjective feelings and opinions over God's objective Word, the duller my heart becomes to hearing His voice. That's why when men approach me with, "How do I hear God speaking to me?" my answer is often something like, "Repent of your porn, smoking, rage, lust, greed, alcohol or drug habits."

You get the point. God speaks constantly using a myriad of venues. When you struggle hearing God, then answer this question, "What voices am I listening to that are drowning out His?" When God goes silent you are most likely the reason, not God.

I've seen once-godly men poisoned by the voices of politics, sports, music, weak friends, Internet searches, books, and false doctrine. Brother, the words you invite into your mind matter. Words are not neutral.

Do you want to hear God's voice? Repent of **habitual neglect** and start forming new rhythms. Remove **deafening agents** from your life and start obeying God's Word- not the Grace Doctrine heresy that promotes a Jell-O-Jesus-effeminate-God who lets people do whatever they want without consequence! Pastors who promote this fantasy are detached from reality, are contradicting the costly grace of God, and should be terminated for heresy and released without severance. It's that serious. The world's deafening scream easily distracts us from God's quiet whisper: *"After the earthquake came a fire, but the Lord was not in the fire. And after the fire came a gentle whisper" (1 Kings 19:12).*

Fight against the deafening screams of our subjective world and listen to the whisper of your King.

Second, Jesus said (Matthew 13:15) that some have "closed their eyes". Unlike the loss of hearing due to habitual neglect over time, closing one's eyes to God is a **decisive act of the will.** Where habitual neglect affects my life in the future, closing my eyes (Shutting out God) immediately affects my heart. We make choices every day. Those choices affect us more than we might admit. Where habitual neglect affects my future, closing my eyes shuts God out now. Do you see the difference? One affects my future over time; one determines my present situation.

What harmful things do you watch? What news stations are causing you to hate other people and political groups that Jesus (wait for it) loves and died for (John 3:16)? Be watchful against biases formed from the news you watch and read. Guard your screens from pornographic images that get stored in your memory banks? There's no "Delete" button. You can't clear your history. What are you watching on social media, the movies, or television? Your obedience today matters!

Where have you turned your back on God's voice? When was the last time you said, "No!" to His whisper? When have you knowingly disobeyed God's Word? What was the last sin you dove headlong into? The psalmist wrote, *"They* **close up** *their callous hearts..." (Psalm 17:10 NIV).* Jesus also said, *"Blessed are the pure in heart, for they will see God" (Matthew 5:8).*

Maybe you are struggling to see God through the darkened lens of sin. Stop looking at darkness, turn back to God, and feel again! Cut away the calluses! Rip off the blindfold! The more apathetic to sin you are, the thicker your heart calluses will be. The greatest sign of discipleship is our struggle against sin. What I celebrated in my years before Christ I now fight for victory against. It's the struggle to resist that prevents our heart from becoming calloused. We sin. It's the reality of life on this dark planet. Fight against it. Declare war!

Cut away any sin threatening to form a callus before it gets ripped off and exposed. Once ripped off you'll be forced to publicly deal with your darkness while trying to stop the bleeding. It ain't pretty. We've seen it far too many times. I once ripped a callus off my hand during a workout on the ninety-fifth out of one hundred pull-ups. Believe me when I say that I forgot the muscle pain, sweat in my eyes, and the last five pull-ups. All attention was immediately focused on the bloody crater in my palm!

When hidden sin is exposed all your attention goes to stop the bleeding and fix the pain. The good news is that where a callus once prevented pain, the exposed crater in my hand was a reminder that I could feel again. Sometimes, God in his great love, rips the callus off to expose a dark secret to the light—a heart attack, an overdose, a divorce, a prison sentence, job loss— may be the last chance to fix your heart. Do not waste the opportunity to change your life.

Cut away all calluses in your life. Be aggressive about it. Confess it from the rooftops. Repent. Turn. Get help now. Grind them off by forming healthy habits. Or, wait until your secret is exposed and you're staring at a bleeding crater on your hand (or life) that your apathy once covered. Do you want that for your marriage? Do you want that for your reputation? Do you want that when people hear your name? Me either!

Strengthen Your Grip
Small Group Exercise

In the movie, *The Secret Life of Walter Mitty*, Time Magazine's motto was beautifully described as, "To see the world, things dangerous to come to, to see behind walls, draw closer, to find each other, and to feel. That is the purpose of life." Which of these stirs your innermost being? Where do you long to feel again?

In Matthew 13:13-15 Jesus said, "Though seeing, they do not see; though hearing, they do not hear or understand. In them is fulfilled the prophecy of Isaiah: 'You will be ever hearing but never understanding; you will be ever seeing but never perceiving. For this people's heart has become calloused; they hardly hear with their ears, and they have closed their eyes. Otherwise they might see with their eyes, hear with their ears, understand with their hearts and turn, and I would heal them.'" What insights did you gather about this verse and fighting apathy?

What is the difference between callous and callus? How are the two similar? What is threatening the most to harden your heart?

Frederick Douglass rightly said, "It is easier to build strong children than to repair broken men." Where do you need to step up your game for those who love you the most? Where have you been apathetic towards them?

72

SHARPEN YOUR FACE
The Eye of the Tiger

"You are never a great man when you have more mind than heart."
~Beauchene

A continual dripping on a rainy day and a quarrelsome wife are alike; to restrain her is to restrain the wind or to grasp oil in one's right hand. Iron sharpens iron, and one man sharpens another. (ESV)
~Proverbs 27:15-17

"Rising up, back on the street did my time, took my chances. Went the distance, now I'm back on my feet just a man and his will to survive. So many times, it happens too fast, you trade your passion for glory. Don't lose your grip on the dreams of the past, you must fight just to keep them alive. It's the eye of the tiger, it's the thrill of the fight, rising up to the challenge of our rival. And the last known survivor stalks his prey in the night and he's watching us all with the eye of the tiger."
~The Band, Survivor
Song, "Eye of the Tiger"

We opened this chapter with the 1982 hit song, *Eye of the Tiger* by the band, Survivor. *Eye of the Tiger* was released for the movie, Rocky III. I can hear the electric guitar intro still, "Dint...dint, dint, dint...dint, dint, dint...dint, dint, dinnnnnn!"

The Eye of the Tiger takes me back to my late teens and early twenties before life had taken its toll. I was single, untamed, a little arrogant, and had the eye of the tiger. A quarter century later with a wife, adult sons, and "dad bod", I have to fight just to get a disappointing, "Dint...dint, dint, dinnnnnnnnn!"

But it's worth it. It's worth **living** every day of your life.

How many guys reading this are alive but not living? They're in a rut. Life has robbed them of the eye of the tiger. If that's you, then take it back!

It's easy to see the apathy in the eyes of a man who has given up. It's even easier to see it in the lives of those he loves. I knew my 90-year-old, Portuguese,

73

firecracker of a Grandpa was close to death when he shared, "Cleaning the leaves out of the rain gutters (while standing on the roof) is all I have to live for now."

He died three years later.

Your face is a billboard. It advertises how well you've handled what life's thrown your way. If you want the world to feel the weight of who you are and want the world to see the light in your eyes, then listen up.

Your face matters!

It tells a story. Just listen to these face idioms.

If I'm sad, then I have **a long** face.

If I'm guilty, it is **written** all over my face.

If I'm frustrated, I'm **blue** in the face.

The best liars do it with **a straight face.**

If I want to be deceptive, I put on a **poker** face.

If I'm embarrassed, I have **egg** on my face.

And if my dignity is stripped, I **lose** face.

Relationships affect our face. Think about how your three closest relationships affect your face—your countenance. Your wife should be number one on that list, then family members and closest buddies. Each man is responsible for his choices but consider the power of each relationship. Those closest to us influence us by making us better or worse, sharper or duller, smarter or dumber, more stable or insecure, stronger or weaker, more of a finisher or quitter, and closer to Jesus or further from Him.

Do you want to change your face? Change your relationships. It's that simple. Get around people that sharpen you. Befriend people who possess the eye of the tiger.

"Dint...dint, dint, dint...dint, dint, dint...dint, dint, dinnnnnn!"

I Don't Like His Face

A story is told about when newly elected President of the United States, Abraham Lincoln, was selecting his Cabinet. A certain man's name was brought to him over and over, but each time Lincoln rejected this highly recommended man. Exasperated his Chief of Staff questioned, "This man is the most qualified man we've presented. Why do you keep rejecting him?"

Lincoln, who is known in history as the ugliest man to ever hold the Presidential office, shot back, "I don't like his face!"

. . .

"But sir", his Chief of Staff responded, "No man can be responsible for his face."

"After forty, every man is responsible for his face!" Lincoln rebutted.

How is your face, friend? What does your countenance portray? Does your face reflect that you need an attitude adjustment?

A better question may be what are you doing about it?

Harvard University's Grant Study

Harvard University's Grant Study was a longitudinal study of 268 physically and mentally healthy white American male college sophomores at Harvard University who were born between 1919-1924.

George Vaillant was the study director tracking the lives of these 268 men over the past 75 years. Information was gathered about their mental and physical health, career enjoyment, retirement experience, and marital quality. The goal of the study was to identify predictors of healthy aging in men. Each man was evaluated every two years by questionnaires, information from their physicians, and personal interviews.

Of the 31 men in the study who were deemed **incapable** of forming intimate relationships, only four were alive in 2014. In other words, the men who isolated themselves from others died much sooner! But of those better at forming relationships, over one-third were still alive in 2014.

From his research Vaillant concluded, "It was the capacity for intimate relationships that predicted the flourishing aspects of these men's lives." In case after case the secret formula for a long and full life is the capacity for intimacy combined with persistence, discipline, order, and dependability. In other words, the men who could be affectionate towards people and organized about things had very enjoyable lives.

Wow! Did you get that?

Relationships matter in forging a great and full life. Change how you do relationships and change your life. Change your relationships and change your face!

Get Out of My Face

Probably the most often quoted Bible verse for men is Proverbs 27:17. I regularly partner with a nationally known organization called Iron Sharpens Iron Men's Conferences. Its name was inspired by that proverb. Here are several popular translations of Proverbs 27:17.

> Iron sharpeneth iron; so a man sharpeneth the countenance of his friend.
> ~King James Version

> As iron sharpens iron, so a man sharpens the countenance of his friend.
> ~New King James Version

> As iron sharpens iron, so one person sharpens another.
> ~New International Version

> As iron sharpens iron, so one man sharpens another.
> ~New American Standard Version

> Iron sharpens iron, and one man sharpens another.
> ~English Standard Version

Each translation sounds great and manly but what do they mean? What does it look like to sharpen someone? How do you know if you are being sharpened? How do you know if you are sharpening someone else? When men sharpen each other, what do they do? How does sharpening happen in the jungles of real life?

We can find a clue by researching the original language—Hebrew. The word for "countenance," used in the King James Version or in the other translations listed above, is the Hebrew word **pene**. The word **pene** literally means "face".

Expositor's Bible Commentaries describes this strange word: "The word **pene** must mean here the personality or character of an individual. *The Talmud*, the body of Jewish civil and ceremonial law and legend comprising the Mishnah and the Gemara, applied it to two students sharpening each other."

Pene is what happens when two or more people challenge each other to better themselves in some way, shape, or form. It's getting around people who make us better. Countenance is how you carry yourself. It's how you portray yourself to those around you. It's the attitude you project. A clearer translation of Proverbs 27:17 would be, "As iron sharpens iron so one man sharpens another's face in a way that transforms his countenance into the eye of a tiger." Maybe not the "eye of the tiger" part, but you get the idea.

Who is sharpening your face? Who is changing your outlook for the better? Who is challenging you to step up to the best version of yourself?

Myth One: Legend of Two Swords

There are, however, a few problems with Proverbs 27:17. The first is that men wrongly communicate an illustration of two swords somehow sharpening each other. Not only is this an inaccurate translation of the proverb, it's not how blades get sharp. I've been sharpening knives to a hair-shaving razor's edge since I was five years old, and I have **never** used two knives to sharpen each other.

Sharpening requires the cutting edge and the sharpening agent. That's it. The blade requires a harder surface in order to break off, sharpen, and hone it to a razor's edge.

I will often sharpen multiple knives in one setting using the same sharpening agent to do so. Sometimes I'll use a "steel" to hone up the blade for immediate use. A steel is a rod of at least a foot long that is made of a metal, graphite, diamond, or other extremely hard element. I use the steel to hone the blade while butchering an animal. It's a short-term fix.

I prefer to use a three-step approach using three distinct sharpening agents to bring a knife from dull to hair-shaving sharp. I have used actual stones, graphite bars, and most recently—belts. These three steps transition the blade from coarsely sharp, to hair-shave sharpened, and ultimately honed to near razor's edge.

In the first step, the coarse stone knocks off the dull blade, creating a sharp yet jagged edge that is easily viewed under a microscope. This could be like one buddy calling another out on some unwise behavior. It is rough, jagged, and blunt force. It gets the job done but more than a blunt confrontation is needed for a healthy friendship.

The second step takes the jagged irregularities away leaving a smooth edge. At this point, the blade can shave hair but its edge is still jagged under a microscope, and won't endure under constant use. Masculine friendships usually get to this point and fall short of the final process. They fail to consistently, strategically, connect to sharpen over time.

And the final step hones the blade to a razor-sharp shine. A man is honed to a razor's edge by consistent gatherings with other men over a long period of time. Sin's propensity is to dull the best of men, and we need Christian men to regularly pour into our lives.

Sharpening relationships work in much the same way. One person is sharpened while the other does the sharpening. How many times have you called a friend because you needed wise counsel, encouragement, or challenge? How many times have you been called for the same? Relationships work that way. When we are weak, we lean on the strength of those closest to us. When we are strong, we offer that strength to those in need. Strong men sharpen other men.

The best relationships are those that do this mutually and even simultaneously. The worst relationships are those that never sharpen each other. The dangerous relationships are those where one is almost always the sharpener and the other only gets sharpened. I call those codependent relationships, which are usually toxic and need to be terminated.

Myth Two: Proverb 27 Problem

There may be a problem with Proverbs 27 that you need to wrestle to the ground and decide on for yourself. Hebrew poetry known as Parallelism is used throughout the study of Proverbs 27. Unlike our modern American society where over 90% of the population is literate, well over 90% of people during Old and New Testaments times were *illiterate*. We live in a visual, literate, world today, but the ancients lived in an oral, illiterate one. Hardly anyone owned or had even touched a book! Passing scripture to other generations was mostly done orally through the means of memorization.

Parallelism was one way of doing this. Over three-fourths of the Old Testament was written in poetic form. That's a lot! In Hebrew parallelism one line either explains the next or describes it in a slightly different way. In Proverbs 27 every two or three verses are linked together by parallel (or similar) statements. This is consistent throughout the book of Proverbs.

Here's the context in which Proverb 27:17 was probably read if verses 15-17 are indeed forms of parallelism: *"A continual dripping on a rainy day and a quarrelsome wife are alike; to restrain her is to restrain the wind or to grasp oil in one's right hand. Iron sharpens iron, and one man sharpens **another**."*

The "another" who is being sharpened by a man might be his wife! She in turn, is also the primary face-sharpening person in his life! I concur that men sharpen the faces of other men as well, but looking only at context, a strong case can be made that the author was writing about the husband-wife relationship. Think about it. Besides your wife (for those who are married), who is the primary sharpener in your life?

Exactly.

If she isn't, maybe she should be!

Darrin Patrick, author of *The Dudes Guide to Manhood* wrote about our wives; "She will remind you of your greatness and your weakness, the glory and the gore. This will crush you and heal you. She will be holy **sandpaper** in your life, rubbing off the things that keep you from being the man you are called to be."

In the context of our discussion, Patrick's quote caught my attention, especially after receiving the Work Sharp Knife and Tool Sharpener as a present from my son. It sharpens with three distinct "sandpaper" belts of varying coarseness. Here is the product description; *"The Work Sharp Knife and Tool Sharpener is an innovative **abrasive** belt sharpening system that combines flexible premium **abrasive belts** and precision sharpening guides to give you the sharpest blades with professional results."*

Whether you call it sandpaper or an abrasive belt, you get the point. Strong wives thrive on grinding away the dull parts of our life to get to our best version. The passion a strong woman brings to a marriage is truly a gift from God, even though it doesn't always feel that way. Maybe your wife is more of a sand **blaster** than sandpaper. Thank God for her strength to sharpen you.

The best wives call out our best. The worst are passive doormats. One reason we live in a world of weak males is because women are weaker than ever before in history. In his book, *Laugh Your Way to a Better Marriage,* Mark Gungor compares modern women to those of the Wild West/Victorian Age who tamed the west with their powerful faith in Jesus. Unlike what you see in western movies, it wasn't six shooters that won the west. It was powerful Christian women who refused to compromise their faith to attract a husband. Gungor writes, "(Too) many modern-day women are more desperate than strong, more devoid of self-esteem than confident. If these women had been the ones who headed west (freely having sex and willingly caring for deadbeat [males] without requiring proper behavior), these men would never have changed dispositions."

Behind most strong men are strong—not weak—women.

Gas Station Submission

Our world needs stronger women. Strong women are submissive. It takes a strong woman to trust her man. They know the power they have and use it strategically. Our modern churches understand marital "submission" all wrong. A Roman soldier of the first century knew that "submission" was a military word that implied a chain of command, where subordinates had a voice, but the ultimate decision rested on the ranking officer.

Submission was, and still is, strategic. Submission is a powerful tool in a marriage where the husband is strong and trustworthy, and the wife is strong enough to trust his leadership. Modern women get bent out of shape, preachers cower from the pulpit, and men shrink back from their God-ordained role as the family leader because of the misinterpretations of this word.

Submission is an attitude that says, "I trust you and will push you to lead." Within the marriage covenant, men are not called to an attitude of submission. Nor are they called to totalitarian lordship. Men are commissioned by God to the consistent **action of sacrifice** on behalf of those they lead. Submission and sacrifice work in harmony to form a healthy household balance. Women, on the other hand, are called by God to the **attitude of submission**—the joyful empowerment of their husband to lead. Note the emboldened terms. Christian marriage is the glorious meshing of two powerful people working in rhythmic harmony with an attitude of submission (wife) and the action of sacrifice (husband).

One of the best descriptions of biblical submission I ever heard came from an anonymous preacher (probably afraid of what would happen if people discovered who he was) who said, "Men are the head of the household! Women, you're the neck!" I love that! It's so true. Innumerable times Shanna saw what I didn't and helped me navigate our family to higher ground.

Someday I will write a book called, *Beside Every Good Man* with the subtitle; *Is a Great Woman!*

Here is my favorite story of biblical submission. I don't know where I heard it or if it's even true, but I love the story. In the 80's First Lady Barbara and President George H. W. Bush were driving across Texas to their home. As the story goes, in a remote part of Texas President Bush had to stop for a restroom break and ordered the full Presidential motorcade to pull into the nearest gas station. President Bush got out of the limousine and went to the restroom. When he returned to the car, he was shocked to see his wife, the First Lady, engaged in a lively conversation with the gas station attendant.

When Barbara climbed into the limousine the President questioned her, "Why did you get out of the limousine to talk to that gas station attendant?"

The First Lady smiled, "It was the strangest thing. When I watched him pumping our gas, I recognized him instantly. He was my high school sweetheart, the first love of my life!"

Laughing, the President said, "How amusing that the First Lady to the most powerful man in the world dated a man who is now a lowly gas station attendant!"

Smirking, she quickly put him in his place, "George, that may be true, but if I would have married him, he'd be the current President of the United States of America!"

That, my friends, is a strong, submissive, woman!

Just Kitchen Knives

Shanna and I started dating on October 29, 1991 and were married on August 1, 1992. I've been faithful to her ever since. Our marriage hasn't been easy. We're strong people and have fought more than our share of battles, often with each other. She has been—by far—the greatest sharpening agent in my life. She is my best friend.

She says the same about me.

She calls me out. When I've failed or have been less than the best version of myself, she is the first to let me know. She's unrelenting! She's committed to me living out my best version, as I am to her. After she trained me to put the toilet lid down after going to the bathroom, she moved on to my wardrobe. Twenty-five years later she's working on my diet, sleep habits, priorities, and time management. No one calls me out like she does. I'd never allow it. And I'm a better man because I have a strong woman as my wife.

She calls me in. During our lifetime we've had loss, suffering, and tragedy. It is during those times that I'm tempted to shrink back and avoid the hard conversations and personal confrontations. She calls me into those tough situations that men have to deal with, but which I would have avoided as a single male.

She calls me up. Shanna believes in me like no other. She sees greatness in me that no one else sees. She is unrelenting as she calls me to greatness, even if I don't want to climb. Men desperately need a wife wise enough to submit and strong enough to call them up to their full potential in Christ.

But it works both ways.

Several years ago, some female teachers in a Christian school voiced their negative opinions to prevent me coming to their school as their spiritual renewal speaker. Here's why. I brought some hunting knives to illustrate my iron sharpens iron point that I explained earlier in the chapter. I can't remember what I said but they were concerned that my knife illustration was too "male-biased" and the young ladies needed more energy directed their way. Without communicating to me about this, they simply stopped inviting me to speak. Until recently. After several years, I was invited back to that school and Proverbs 27:17 was my teaching passage. Getting the elephant out of the room, I shared that this time I'd give equal focus to both young men and women. I openly shared that in our household I was the primary cook and that Shanna would starve to death without me, which is true by the way. I literally have a carrying case for my favorite cooking and butchering knives. When I opened the case and proudly displayed my two favorite "kitchen" knives, the room altogether gasped —at both shimmering twelve-inch blades! The crowd erupted in applause. I assured them they weren't hunting but kitchen knives! It was epic although I'm not so sure the subversive women teachers appreciated the applause.

The point is this—when it comes to relationships two blades can't sharpen each other. They aren't made for that. They are made to cut. A blade needs a sharpening agent of some kind to stay razor sharp.

Sharpening occurs when a blade interfaces with a blade sharpening agent. Sometimes Shanna sharpens me. Other times, I sharpen her. It's the same with the handful of men who have permission to sharpen my face. Sometimes I sharpen them. Other times they sharpen me. I am honed to my best version when I am meeting weekly with men I deeply trust, want the best for me, and strategically sharpen me.

Do you want the eye of the tiger? Do you long for the faith of a child? Sharpen your wife's face. Demand that she does the same for you. Find other men with the guts to sharpen you—to call you out, call you in, and call you up.

Strengthen Your Grip
Small Group Exercise

If men tend to be good thinkers but struggle with intimacy, how could that cause a shorter life span?

What new insights did you gain form Proverbs 27:17? What does it mean to sharpen one's face?

Proverbs 27:15-17 (ESV) says, "A continual dripping on a rainy day and a quarrelsome wife are alike; to restrain her is to restrain the wind or to grasp oil in one's right hand. Iron sharpens iron, and one man sharpens another." How does your wife sharpen you more than any other person? What happens when you refuse to be sharpened?

In what ways do other men sharpen you that your wife never could? What things do they ask you that she probably never will? What ways do they push you that she most likely will not?

THE WALKING DEAD
Waking the Dead

"The only difference between a rut and the grave is the size of the hole."
~Unknown

"Welcome to the planet, welcome to resistance."
~The Band Switchfoot
Song, "Dare you to Move"

"The world has been wrong about you. They've hated your glory—just as the Evil One hates the glory of God. But we need your gift. Come forth."
~John Eldredge
Waking the Dead

Walkers

A while back I got into a television show called *The Walking Dead*. Don't judge. I love the psychology of surviving an apocalyptic event such as this—the "Walkers" were a bonus. *The Walking Dead* is about how the power of the mind during a catastrophic event causes some to collapse and fall victim to their surroundings, and others to adapt, adjust, and survive. It's a show about the fragile state of the human condition.

We've seen this, in part, during the COVID-19 pandemic crisis. Penning these words in the midst of the pandemic (May 2020) and our state of Oregon is in the early phases of opening commerce. I've found it fascinating to watch how various people, groups, and leaders are dealing with the current way of life. Some have used this unprecedented time to courageously step into a better version of themselves where others have hidden, allowing fear to bring out the worst in them.

For those who haven't seen the show, it's about a pandemic, somewhat similar except this one leads to an apocalyptic event. But this is a unique kind of virus, which kills its victims by quickly turning them into walkers—zombies— the walking dead. The only way a walker can be killed is by a traumatic incident to the brain such as a bullet, knife, or blunt force cranial event.

The "Walkers" kill healthy humans and animals (or any living thing they can catch) with their infected bite and often ripping them to shreds as the victims scream in horror! Once bitten, a human is infected, eventually dies, and is quickly regenerated as a zombie. The only medical solution is the merciful death in the form of a massive cranial event.

Reflecting upon the Walkers themselves brought me to an interesting conclusion. First, even when wounded or dismembered, they show no signs of pain. In this zombie-like state they lose all physical and emotional feelings. Second, they're walking but not living. They are dead but masquerading as living. Third, they make noise but have no voice. They grunt, growl, and groan, but have no ability to communicate. Fourth, they seem to wander without purpose. They aimlessly follow sounds but have no idea where they are going or why. Lastly, all were once human but lost their soul after the infection turned them into a Walker. They resemble humans but are controlled by a mysterious zombie force.

The similarity between weak men today and Walkers from the television series is frightening. I hear stories about zombie-like, apathetic, weak males almost daily. There's a reason you can't spell apathetic without being pathetic! The only difference between the two is that the Walker was transformed into his state from an attack, but the weak man is the product of personal choice.

The zombie male shows no concern for those he should care about the most. He wounds others by his callousness but doesn't seem to care. He's breathing but not living. He masquerades as a man yet remains a mere male. He makes a lot of noise but doesn't back it up with action. He makes promises he doesn't keep. He bears children he refuses to raise. He starts jobs he can't finish. He makes bold claims he never fulfills. He has no voice where he should carry heaviest influence. He's lost.

Have I just described you? Are you a male or a man? Did you surrender your Man Card years ago? If so, it's time to get it back. A male can't be transformed into a man until he acknowledges his real state, turns, and acts as a man. Remember, a man is as a man does.

Change your world today. Be resurrected as a man!

Deer Alarm Clock

I was speaking loudly at a men's event in the Willamette Valley, Oregon. The struggle when teaching to any outside group is speaking with enough authority to be heard over the outdoors distractions. Because I believe adamantly that apathy is the greatest battle a man will ever fight, I speak on this topic as often, and as loud as possible.

At the end of the second day a pastor approached me with, "Jim, can I give you some feedback?" That phrase usually precedes harsh criticism, so I braced for impact. But his story shocked me and affirmed everything we've been fighting for. Here is my best recollection of his story.

"The day we arrived at camp one of my guys got deathly sick with food poisoning. All he could do was sleep, vomit, and repeat. After your seminar, which we both attended, he shared with the men from our church that his life had been changed. He recommitted his life to Christ and was going to reengage with his children. When asked which seminar he attended he said, 'It was something like *"How to engage in your children after divorce"* with a guy named Jim Ramos. He was reading some statistic about absent fathers and I realized I was one of them.'"

The pastor continued, "the amazing thing was how he ended up at your seminar. He was in his tent sleeping off his food poisoning when a deer—**a deer**—wandered into his tent and **woke him up!** In a sleep stupor he staggered out of his tent and followed the loudspeaker voice to your presentation!"

A deer?

Are you kidding me! Do you think fighting apathy matters to God? I remember that presentation clearly. I also remember going on a rant about those statistics and thinking, "I usually don't go off like this. I wonder why I'm so fired up today?"

Here are those statistics. I think we'll all agree that although these are older statistics, they've gotten worse, not better. Most of the statistics are from the 2000 and 2010 US censuses.

Twenty-four million children will go to bed without a biological father.

Sixty-six percent of children are not expected to live with their father through **age 18.**

Next is the statistic that woke up the man in our story; The American Academy of Pediatrics survey said that half of all children from divorce will not see their father for *over a year!* I'm an adult child from divorce, but my Dad never lost touch with his kids—ever. He could've written a book on staying engaged with his children after divorce. Do you see the ramifications here? Over half of the children who get the "It's Not Your Fault" divorce speech from their parents are severely punished by an absent male disguising himself as a parent!

Half!

An Uphill Battle

Men, we are fighting an uphill battle to reclaim the manhood that society has stolen. It's time to take it back! Resist the temptation to become callous. Join us in the fight for men and those they love. Become one of the thousands of men from around the world who listen to the Men in the Arena podcast, grow as a man through the Men in the Arena Facebook forum, and refuse to succumb to the neutered voices trying to silence the authority God has given.

The task is overwhelming. The climb is steep. How do you ascend the steepest of slopes? One step at a time!

Fighting apathy is a daily battle. Climbing up the steep and rugged cliffs of manhood is draining, especially when your legs are on fire from the mountain's resistance. The mountain will always fight back.

Yes!

Strengthen Your Grip
Small Group Exercise

John Eldredge in his great book, Waking the Dead wrote, "The world has been wrong about you. They've hated your glory—just as the Evil One hates the glory of God. But we need your gift. Come forth." What does this mean and why is it so important for men to get it?

In Job 29:2-5, Job laments, "How I long for the months gone by, for the days when God watched over me, when his lamp shone on my head and by his light I walked through darkness! Oh, for the days when I was in my prime, when God's intimate friendship blessed my house, when the Almighty was still with me and my children were around me." You've heard it said of parenting, "Enjoy it while you can. It goes so fast." But life in the arena or raising a family is so exhausting! How do you (or did you) stay close to your kids? How do you stay closer to them now?

Jim wrote, "The zombie male shows no concern for those he should care about the most. He wounds others by his callousness but doesn't seem to care. He's breathing but not living. He masquerades as a man yet remains a mere male. He makes a lot of noise but doesn't back it up with action. He makes promises he doesn't keep. He bears children he refuses to raise. He starts jobs he can't finish. He makes bold claims he never fulfills." Are any of these hitting close to home? What can you do to make it right?

What can you do to prevent any of the above from ever happening? What does a strong man do to prevent calluses from forming over his heart? How do you stay engaged?

PART III

THE SUMMIT: PURSUING GOD PASSIONATELY

GOD HUNTERS
Pursue the Right Trophy

Not that I have already obtained it or have already become perfect, but I **press on** *so that I may lay hold of that for which also I was laid hold of by Christ Jesus. Brethren, I do not regard myself as having laid hold of it yet; but one thing I do: forgetting what lies behind and reaching forward to what lies ahead, I* **press on** *toward the goal for the prize of the upward call of God in Christ Jesus.*
~Philippians 3:12-14

"To have found God and still to pursue Him is the soul's paradox of love."
~A.W. Tozer
The Pursuit of God

"The verb dioko, translated here and in verse 14 'press on', is a hunting word meaning 'I pursue'; it is also used of foot-racing. It is a strong expression for active and earnest endeavor. It is correlative with 'take hold' in a number of passages in the sense of 'pursue and overtake', 'chase and capture'."
~Ralph Martin
Tyndale New Testament Commentaries

I'm a storyteller. Some stories are great and others, well, not so great. I love using stories and objects to illustrate the point I'm trying to make. Not only do they keep men engaged, they drive home the point trying to be made. The story I'm about to share is an epic story of stories.

A trophy sits on an adjacent bookshelf as I'm writing this chapter. I received it after my senior football season at Santa Clara University for being named the "Most Courageous" of my eighty-plus teammates. Its marble base is missing, but it still stands there to remind me of an unforgettable event.

As the Youth Pastor of El Morro Church of the Nazarene in the 1990's I was speaking to my youth group about Philippians 3:7-8, which says, *"But whatever things were gain to me, those things I have counted as loss for the sake of Christ. More than that, I count all things to be loss in view of the surpassing value of knowing Christ Jesus my Lord, for whom I have suffered the loss of all things, and count them but rubbish so that I may gain Christ."*

On an eight-foot table in front of me stood dozens of trophies I'd earned over my athletic career, none of which were Participation Trophies. They sat there waiting to be memorialized as the climax of the night's message and my most unforgettable sermon illustration of all time.

I explained where I'd earned some of the taller ones: High School "Athlete of the Year" as a junior, and another for the same thing my senior year. I went down the line, explaining trophy after trophy until their glassy eyes told me they were bored, which was about three trophies if I'm honest!

Then I opened my Bible, read Philippians 3:7-8, and explained that all our trophies fail in comparison to having a relationship with God. Then I did something I hope they've never forgotten. I walked to the end of the table and lifted it high in the air, sending every trophy crashing onto the floor in an explosion of marble, wood and plastic!

It was a message I'll never forget. I can't speak for the teens!

I had spent the early part of my life pursuing early trophies that were only as strong as the floor I smashed them on. If only I had spent the first two decades of life pursuing the trophy that never fades away, can be destroyed, or sadly disappoints.

The apex of manhood (of mankind for that matter) is pursuing God. It's the summit. It's the top. It's truly where a man discovers that his best version is far beyond whatever he thought it was without Christ. Do you want the world to witness the best version of you? Pursue God passionately and regularly for the rest of your life.

Dioko

A few verses later, the Apostle Paul drove home his point in Philippians 3:12-14; *"Not that I have already obtained it or have already become perfect, but I press on (dioko) so that I may lay hold of that for which also I was laid hold of by Christ Jesus. Brethren, I do not regard myself as having laid hold of it yet; but one thing I do: forgetting what lies behind and reaching forward to what lies ahead, I press on (dioko) toward the goal for the prize of the upward call of God in Christ Jesus."*

. . .

Did you notice the Greek word **dioko** in parentheses? **Dioko** is the Greek word the New American Standard Bible (NASB) twice translates as "press on". In the *Tyndale New Testament Commentaries Study of the Book of Philippians*, Ralph Martin writes that this word literally means, "I pursue". The verb is translated in verses 12 and 14 as "press on". *Dioko* had a two-fold meaning for the Greeks. First, it was a hunting word meaning "I pursue or stalk". Second **dioko** was also used in **foot racing** to describe chasing after or pursuing as in a race.

My personal understanding of the word **dioko** inspired the original name of our organization (2011-2017), The Great Hunt for God.

Pursue the greatest Prize in the universe. A man may pursue many trophies in life, but if the Creator of the universe isn't **by far** his most important, his priorities are way out of order. Too many "Christian" men do second things first, forsaking the God of the universe as preeminent in their life. This reminds me of a story.

Mendota Nights

I love hunting ducks. One hunt before my sons were old enough to hunt stands out, and not because we shot a lot of ducks. In fact, we only shot a handful between the five of us that day. It was actually a miserable hunt involving humiliation, hypothermia, a knee injury, and one damaged shotgun! Here's what happened. My hunting buddy Bob and I were going to hunt the Mendota Wildlife Refuge with his son-in law (who was recovering from a total knee reconstruction), his son, and a young man from my youth group.

We packed up our gear and guns and drove the three hours to the refuge, arriving at 10:00 the night before the hunt. We parked in the middle of three lines of trucks and about 40 vehicles back. Duck hunters call this the notorious "Sweat Line" because you're sweating to get into the refuge first in order to get the most desirable hunting spots. It's a redneck race that you have to see to believe. Sometimes truth is stranger than fiction!

The young guys decided to sleep under the Suburban, while Bob and I made the bucket seats our beds for the night. I spent a sleepless night trying to fall asleep sitting up, but the young guys had it worse. Sometime in the early morning hours it started pouring, soaking them in their sleeping bags. By the time the Sweat Line opened at 4:30 am, they were wet, cold, and exhausted.

· · ·

We waited for the endless lines of vehicles to go through the line, finally received our permits, and sped into the muddy refuge. Arriving in our predetermined parking lot, we reversed our packs to front-facing, loaded the decoy bags on our backs (about three dozen each), grabbed our guns, and ran over a mile in full chest waders down a muddy levee trying to reach our hunting pond before any others.

To add insult to injury it was still raining, blurring our vision as the rain poured down and our sweat mist rose up—fogging up the view from our headlamps!

Just as we reached the pond, Bob's son-in-law re-injured his knee by twisting it in an invisible mud hole. The young man from my youth group tripped while entering the pond and buried his borrowed shotgun barrel three feet into the mud. Exhausted, wet, and cold, we silently set up the decoys in the dark and gathered for our traditional pre-hunt prayer.

Staring at their solemn faces through our blazing headlamps in the darkness and pouring rain, I had an epiphany, "Guys, what if we pursued God the way we are chasing these stupid ducks?"

For that brief moment all eyes lit up the darkness in agreement as we prayed a short prayer that none would soon forget.

Think about the things you pursue—career, children's sports, hobbies, and material wealth. How does your pursuit of God compare to your **financial** investment in these things? How does your **time** investment compare to the time you spend pursuing spiritual things? How about your **heart**? How does your hunger for God compare to your desire to possess the above list?

If your pursuit of God doesn't surpass them all, then you're out of order and will never become the best version of yourself under God. I know it's audacious to use the word "never" to describe a life but hear me out. If you're reading this book you most likely believe in God, and possibly call yourself a "Christian". How am I doing so far?

Good.

If you believe in God, then you also believe that He created you. Let's keep going down this levee. If He created you, then it makes logical sense that He loves you and wants the best for your life. Right? Exactly! Because He created you, loves you, and wants you to be the best version of you, He must have some kind of plan for you.

. . .

This elusive "plan", however, would have to be twofold. There would be a **general** plan for all of humanity who commit to the ways of God, and a **personal** plan uniquely designed for you. God gave us the general plan through the Word of God—the Bible. All who are followers of Jesus should live in ruthless obedience to that plan.

Your **personal** plan requires obedience to the Bible while searching out the answer to two key questions in life, which is explained in the following chapters. Underline this: *unless you are obedient to God's general plan in the Bible, you'll struggle to uncover His personal plan, or mission, for your life.* I recognize the boldness and truth of this statement. I hope you do as well.

Here's the bottom line. In our masculine way of looking at life through compartmentalized lenses, it's critical for us to understand that *God isn't interested in being a part of your life.* Did you hear that? God doesn't desire simply being a **part of your life.**

He wants to be all of it. He wants all of you. And he deserves it since He bought it on the cross!

When asked what the greatest commandment was, Jesus quickly responded, *"You shall love the Lord your God with all your heart, and with all your soul, and with all your mind, and with all your strength" (Mark 12:30).*

How much of your life does God have? How much of your time? How much of your money? How much of your resources? How much of your unique skill set? How much of your heart is His?

If you've answered those questions honestly, then you're ready to answer life's two most important questions: **Who am I?** and **Why am I Here?** Keep reading if you dare!

Strengthen Your Grip
Small Group Exercise

What false trophies is your heart pursuing before Jesus Christ? What do those who love you the most, pray the most passionately for? Is there an area of your life where you struggle to keep Jesus first?

A.W. Tozer in, *The Pursuit of God* wrote, "To have found God and still to pursue Him is the soul's paradox of love." What does this mean to you?

In Philippians 3:12-14 the Apostle Paul wrote, "Not that I have already obtained it or have already become perfect, but I press on so that I may lay hold of that for which also I was laid hold of by Christ Jesus. Brethren, I do not regard myself as having laid hold of it yet; but one thing I do: forgetting what lies behind and reaching forward to what lies ahead, I press on toward the goal for the prize of the upward call of God in Christ Jesus." How do you connect with God? What pathways help you connect with God the best?

Do you have a sense of God' personal plan, or mission, for you? If so, what is it? If not, why?

WHO AM I?
Let the World Feel Your Weight

"The questions of who we are and why we are here are far more important
questions than
how to land a great job and make money."
~John and Sam Eldredge
Killing Lions

"Unless you assume a God, the question of life's purpose is meaningless."
~Bertrand Russell
Atheist

"You were shaped to serve God...each of us was uniquely designed, or 'shaped',
to do certain things."
Rick Warren
Purpose Driven Life

Here's the tragic story of a close friend. I've changed a lot of the details to protect his identity and loved ones. He was abused as a child, struggled as a teen, and got his girlfriend pregnant halfway through high school. They were married as teenagers, but their young marriage struggled and ended in divorce. Miraculously he got custody of their two-year-old toddler and newborn daughter. He struggled as a single parent raising two children, so he took a second job working as a fast food restaurant cook. He did all this while taking online courses, and ultimately graduating with his bachelor's degree.

He married a second time, to a wonderful Christian woman, got hired at a local business firm and went back to school—this time real estate—and shortly became a licensed agent. Not to be detoured from his dreams, he enrolled in graduate school and earned a PhD. But adultery ended his second marriage, costing him the relationships with his teenage children.

After marrying his mistress and finishing his first book, he promoted the book by traveling around the country as a motivational speaker, inspiring people to better themselves.

. . .

My buddy had climbed the corporate ladder. He'd made it to the top! But it came at a great cost. He realized he'd paid a great price to climb the corporate ladder and then discovered, to his horror, that it was leaning on the wrong building! On Christmas Day his family found him inside his truck, dead from a self-inflicted wound.

He'd bought the lie—hook, line, and sinker. He left those who loved him with a lot of questions. He was on course to finish strong. Instead he finished wrong. My best guess is that my friend's career had become his identity and when he realized his epic mistake it was too much for him to bear.

His life and tragic death is an example of a man who asked the wrong questions.

What questions are you asking? What is the most important one? Here it is. Are you ready? Don't blink.

Who am I?

Knowing the answer to this question will change your life. Hang on. Here it comes!

Purpose Driven Life

In 2002 Rick Warren wrote his #1 New York Times best seller *The Purpose Driven Life.* The book was so wildly successful that Pastor Rick literally paid his church back for every dollar they'd ever given him. Then he stopped receiving his salary altogether! I love it! The subtitle of the book is *What on earth am I here for?*

If you haven't done so, read that book. Read it after this one. It will change your life. Warren goes deep on some of the things I'll share briefly. Knowing who we are empowers us to live with mission, purpose, and a sense of hope. Matthew Henry wrote, "It ought to be the business every day to prepare for the final day."

But how do you prepare for the final day without direction? It starts with knowing who you are.

To help better understand who you are, let's ask some related questions. God, how did you make me? What unique gifts, abilities, and skills do I bring to the table?

What's the purpose of me?

What hand have I been dealt?

Now, look at your hand. Unless you're like my late Grandpa "Jimmy" Ramos, who lost a finger in a construction accident, most of us have five fingers. *The Purpose Driven Life* outlines five ways God (and life) has shaped us. Imagine each finger on your hand as a letter spelling the word SHAPE.

What's in your hand? What hand has God, life, and personal choices, dealt you? The answer to the question, "Who am I?" is the sum of these five things. Here they are.

SHAPE: Spiritual Gifts

When you became a follower of Jesus, God threw a party (Luke 15:7, 10, and 32). At your salvation party the angels of heaven celebrated, and God gave you some invisible, intangible, presents that the Bible calls "spiritual gifts" (Romans 12:1-8, 1 Corinthians 12:1-31, and 14:1-12). There is much theological debate about what gifts are available, how they are imparted, and when they are given, but hear me out and debate later. These gifts aren't fully developed and may go initially unnoticed until they germinate in your heart, but they're in your hand nonetheless waiting for the day to sprout.

When I was in college, I had a paralyzing fear of public speaking that compelled me to craft a "syllabus routine". On day one of class I'd look over the syllabus. If I saw an oral presentation mentioned **anywhere** on the course outline, I'd politely return the syllabus to the curious professor, smile, and walk out never to return. This happened more than I'd like to admit! In an ironic twist of events, my first job after giving my life to Christ involved the heavy weight of public speaking. And I wasn't good at it. In fact, I was terrible! Then I entered full time ministry! Early on I was appalled that God would call me to do something that I not only feared, but was horrible at.

Over time, much failure, and embarrassing moments, one day I started noticing an encouraging trend—God was using my voice to impact hearts. After years of great practice, patience, and humility, God has brilliantly manifested that gift according to my unique style. The thing I feared the worst, God has used in me the most. I'm amazed by His grace! Whenever someone compliments me at a speaking engagement, I remember my college days, inwardly laugh, and offer a heart-felt, "Thank you."

. . .

Spiritual Gifts tests are different based on the doctrine of the local church or denomination. If your church doesn't have a spiritual gifts test that aligns with their theology, you can find them all over the Internet.

I've discovered that my top three gifts have not changed but God gives fresh gifts in new seasons of life. I take one of these tests every few years just to see what God is doing. When we launched *Men in the Arena,* I was amazed at the gift of **faith** topping my list! This was a first for me and the timing was perfect during a season I needed it the most.

You should know your top three gifts from memory and focus your career and ministry attention on using them to the fullest extent. I shudder when spiritual leaders downplay the gifts. How can we minimize something that the God of the universe gave you in celebration of your return home?

SHAPE: Heart or Passion

In regards to heart, I'm talking about passion. What are you passionate about? What wrecks you? Growing up I watched a cartoon called Popeye the Sailor Man. Created in 1929 by Elzie Segar, Popeye was a short, weak, and bald sailor in love with his oddly named girlfriend—Olive Oyl. Popeye's adversary was a giant of a man named Brutus; whose name was later changed to Bluto. Bluto would harass and abuse Popeye until the battered sailor would proclaim, "That's all I can stand, cuz I can't stand it n'more!"

At that he'd down his can of spinach, exhibit superhuman strength, and the beat down of Bluto would commence. I lived for those Popeye-Moments as a child! What is your Popeye-Moment? What wrecks you? What hill will you die on? That, my friend, is your heart and passion.

In the second century A.D., St. Irenaeus wrote, "The glory of God is man fully alive!" That quote not only changed my life but was the impetus for the conception of Men in the Arena. Every man has a passion. What's yours? Have you lost it? Find it. Let the blood flow hot in your veins once again. Get reacquainted with your life. Repent of anonymity and get in the arena. Turn from your passionless existence and make your life count! Get in the game.

You're not a victim. With God you're a victor. Start acting like one! Your head alone changes nothing, but your head combined with a passionate heart will change your world!

SHAPE: Abilities

A few years back I was the keynote speaker along with ex-NFL quarterback, Jay Shroeder in Tehachapi, California. Jay offered a message of hope as he shared his professional sports experiences. A UCLA graduate, Jay started his professional career in 1979 playing catcher in the minor leagues for the Toronto Blue Jays. Before games Jay would make money by betting opposing players that he could throw a baseball from home plate over the center field fence, over four hundred feet away! He made a lot of money doing this!

He eventually hung up his catcher's mitt and picked up a football helmet, and in 1984 was drafted to the Washington Redskins as a quarterback. He played behind Joe Theismann until one memorable night during a Monday Night Football game, when Joe suffered a career-ending broken leg after a vicious blind side hit from Lawrence Taylor of the New York Giants. Jay won the starting position that year and the next season (1986) led the Redskins to a 12-4 record and NFC title game, where the Giants shut them out 17-0. When Jay was plagued by a shoulder injury the following season, Doug Williams led the Redskins to a Super Bowl XXII championship.

Reflecting on his illustrious career and the strong arm God gave him, Jay stared at his huge Super Bowl ring. Then he said something I'll never forget, "God gives each of us talents and abilities to use for His glory. **I can throw things far.**"

What! Is that it! Is that all you've got Jay? You throw things far? Really! But God has used Jay's strong arm to minister to athletes of every level for the past three decades!

What abilities do you have? No ability is too small for the God who gave it to use mightily!

SHAPE: Personality or Temperament

Hippocrates was a Greek physician who lived between 460–370 BC. He believed certain human moods, emotions, and behaviors were caused by an excess or lack of body fluids: blood, yellow bile, black bile, and phlegm. Disgusting, I know!

These four fluids were the temperamental categories later named Sanguine (blood), Choleric (yellow bile), Melancholic (black bile) and Phlegmatic (phlegm) by Roman physician Claudius Galen (131-201 A.D.).

A lot of fluids have passed under the bridge since then, and we've discovered much more about human temperaments. My first encounter with Hippocrates' theory was in the late 90's when I read a life-changing book by Florence Littauer called, *Personality Plus: How to Understand Others by Understanding Yourself.* In it she modernized these ancient theories by giving them easily relatable adjectives describing each—**popular** Sanguine, **powerful** Choleric, **perfect** Melancholic, and **peaceful** Phlegmatic.

Around that same time, Gary Smalley and John Trent gave these temperament traits the animal names otter, lion, beaver, and golden retriever. Combining them all we have the Popular Otter (Sanguine), Powerful Lion (Choleric), Perfect Beaver (Melancholic), and Peaceful Golden Retriever (Phlegmatic)

As a young man living in the Stress Bubble who was married less than six years, with three children under four years old, Littauer's test equipped me to celebrate the differences of my volunteer team members instead of criticizing them. It changed my ministry perspective and how I related to people.

There are various personality tests out there like Meyer-Briggs, DISC, and Enneagram, but I've found Florence Littauer's *Personality Plus* and John Trent and Gary Smalley's Personality Types Inventory Test are the simplest and most effective in understanding myself and those around me. Both are invaluable resources that are easily found online.

If you haven't done so yet, ask yourself a few preliminary questions. Am I an introvert or extrovert? Do people generally drain or energize me? Am I detail or big-picture oriented? Am I a high energy or relaxed person? Am I a peacemaker or pot-stirrer? Am I the life of the party or a wallflower? My apologies for using the word "flower"!

SHAPE: Experiences

We're a product of our experiences. Good, bad, or ugly, we bring our unique set of ever-expanding experiences to the table. Heraclitus rightly said, "No man ever steps in the same river twice, for it's not the same river and he's not the same man." Our experiences change us. How we handle them determines whether that change is good or bad.

I don't have the answers to why bad things—sometimes evil things—happen to the innocent. I don't know why God intentionally allows such things, or if He does. But one thing I'm convinced of is that God never wastes a hurt. Romans 8:28 is an excellent reminder of this, *"And we know that God causes all things to work together for good to those who love God, to those who are called according to His purpose."*

God uses all our experiences for His glory once we find forgiveness (for ourselves or our violators), healing, and heart reconciliation. Helen Keller, born deaf and blind, truly understood what it was like to be dealt an unfair life, yet she powerfully expressed, "Character cannot be developed in ease and quiet. Only through experience of trial and suffering can the soul be strengthened, ambition inspired, and success achieved."

Have you dealt with your past in a way that frees up your future? Or are you in bondage to a past betrayer or abuser? Unlike the old adage, time will not heal all wounds. You must deal with it. Open wounds are unacceptable for the godly man. Scars are welcomed and appreciated. We offer others healing through our scars, but open wounds must be cauterized sooner rather than later. There are many resources to help you find healing, but my favorite is doing what Jesus admonished followers in Luke 6:27-26:

> *"But I say to you who hear, love your enemies, do good to those*
> *who hate you, bless those who curse you, pray for those who*
> *mistreat you. Whoever hits you on the cheek, offer him the*
> *other also; and whoever takes away your coat, do not*
> *withhold your shirt from him either. Give to everyone who*
> *asks of you, and whoever takes away what is yours, do not*
> *demand it back. Treat others the same way you want them to*
> *treat you. If you love those who love you, what credit is that to*
> *you? For even sinners love those who love them. If you do*
> *good to those who do good to you, what credit is that to you?*
> *For even sinners do the same. If you lend to those from whom*
> *you expect to receive, what credit is that to you? Even sinners*
> *lend to sinners in order to receive back the same amount. But*
> *love your enemies, and do good, and lend, expecting nothing*

in return; and your reward will be great, and you will be sons of the Most High; for He Himself is kind to ungrateful and evil men. *Be merciful, just as your Father is merciful."*

I'll leave you with this truth from Soren Kierkegaard, "Life can only be understood backwards; but it must be lived forwards." We live life looking forward, but we learn from it by looking back.

God never wastes a wound.

Answer the Public

You are the sum of the above five things that determine your SHAPE: Spiritual gifts, Heart or passion, Abilities, Personality or temperament, and Experiences. I don't want to oversimplify the answer to this chapter's title question. The goal of this chapter was to effectively communicate a clear way of understanding who you are. How did we do?

Since entering full time ministry in 1990, I have found no better tool than Rick Warren's SHAPE acrostic to effectively answer the "Who am I?" question. Let the world feel your full weight. Don't try to act like somebody else. Be the most authentic version of **you**. There is no other you and there never will be. When God made you, he broke the mold! Now go and celebrate your SHAPE— who you really are.

We've answered the most important question in life, now it's time to tackle the question most often asked by men.

Strengthen Your Grip
Small Group Exercise

How would you answer the question, "Who am I?" Look at Exodus 4:2 the Lord said to Moses, "What is that in your hand?" What is in your hand? How has God uniquely gifted you?

Psalm 20:4 (ESV) says, *"May he grant you your heart's desire and fulfill all your plans!"* *Other* translations vary slightly but say basically the same thing, that God has a plan for you that you are already passionate about. What are some of your passions? What things wreck you? What things stir you with emotion?

In his wildly popular book, *Purpose Driven Life,* Rick Warren said, "You were shaped to serve God...each of us was uniquely designed, or 'shaped', to do certain things." Take a moment to reflect on what you know about yourself. What is your SHAPE?

- What are your top three **spiritual gifts**?
- What are you passionate about" What ignites your **heart's** fire?
- What natural **abilities** do you possess? What skills have you learned at a high level?
- What kind of **personality** do you have? What is your temperament?
- What **experiences** have you had? What experiences have been forced on you by the choices of others?

WHY AM I HERE?
Position Doubtful

"It's not about you. The purpose of your life is far greater than your own personal fulfillment, your peace of mind, or even your happiness. It's far greater than your family, your career, or even your wildest dreams and ambitions. If you want to know why you were placed on this planet, you must begin with God. You were born by his purpose and for his purpose."
~Rick Warren
Purpose Driven Life

"To think what is true, to sense what is beautiful and to want what is good, hereby the spirit finds purpose of a life in reason."
~Johann Gottfried Herder

"The purpose of life is not to be happy. It is to be useful, to be honorable, to be compassionate, to have it make some difference that you have lived and lived well."
~Ralph Waldo Emerson

In 1932 Amelia Earhart became the first woman to fly solo across the Atlantic Ocean. In July 1937, with Fredrick Noonan as her navigator, she set out to be the first person to fly around the world at the equator. In the Western Pacific, somewhere near New Guinea, she lost her bearings. Her last radio message was, "Position doubtful."

A massive search found nothing but ocean.

Her tragic "loss of position" reminds me of the myriads of once strong men that get lost in the 25-year period of life we call the Stress Bubble. They get up every day and grind it out while passion sputters somewhere between career, raising a family, loving their wives, and (hopefully) serving in the community. Attrition wears them down, grinding away at them day after unrelenting day until once powerful men get lost in the Bubble. Days, months, and years go by until their dreams dissipate into a vague mist of a memory from a past life.

Sadly, many lose their way and fall victim to a mundane life of purposelessness.

Their status becomes, "Position doubtful."

The most popular question others have asked me over the years is "How do I know God's will for my life?"

The only thing worse than not having the answer to these questions is asking the wrong ones. Many have bought the lie that their career and financial portfolio define them. This may be **the** greatest lie whispered in the ear of every man.

What you do does not define who you are! Rather, who you are should define what you do!

Dave Ramsey, creator of the incredibly successful *Financial Peace University* rightly describes our generation as, "The most highly marketed society in the history of the world." I agree. We've been brainwashed into thinking that luxury items are not only wanted but needed for survival. I met with a couple who privately shared that they were in debt up to their eyeballs and struggling badly. But outwardly they "owned" multiple boats, horse trailers, cars, trucks, and cargo trailers; all stored on their two dozen acres. I told them to sell the extras to get out of debt. Wide-eyed the wife said, "We can't sell those things, we **need** them!"

I know of another guy who has more toys that he will ever use. Once he shared his disdain for a monthly boat payment and a boat he never used. I encouraged him to sell the boat and get out of debt.

"I can't sell my boat. That's my stuff!"

What a bunch of bull!

Westminster Shorter Catechism

The Westminster Shorter Catechism was written in 1646 and 1647 by the Westminster Assembly, which was a council of English and Scottish theologians and laymen. It was intended to bring the Church of England into greater conformity with the Church of Scotland. The assembly also produced the Westminster Confession of Faith and the Westminster Larger Catechism.

The purpose of the Shorter Catechism was to educate children and other beginning church attendees about the teachings of the church. The catechism is composed of 107 questions and answers. The most famous of the questions is the first:

.   .   .

Question. What is the chief end of man?

Answer. Man's chief end is to glorify God, and to enjoy Him forever.

Man's chief end is first, to glorify God, and second, to enjoy Him forever. Let's break this down.

To "glorify" something is simply to put it on display for all to see. At Christmas we take a young tree living happily in the Oregon mountains, hack it down, take a picture for social media while doing it, drag it through the forest, throw it in the truck, strap is down tightly, drag it up the stairs, and put it on a stand in front of the largest window in the house!

Poor tree! It had a rough day. But then something glorious happens. We unpack decades worth of our most precious ornaments, and with the utmost care we decorate it with lights, tinsel, and ornaments! I once saw one with lit candles all over it! As the tree's new owners, we literally display the tree in all of its new beauty for the world to see.

We put it on display.

We **glorify** it!

This is the will of God for us, that He puts us on display for the world so that we will **bear witness** of His work in us. Hopefully we won't get chopped down in the process! In other words, we glorify God when we use our God-given SHAPE to bless the world around us, giving God all the credit.

Furthermore, "to enjoy Him forever" simply means to pursue our relationship with God in the way uniquely crafted for us. Our relationship with God on earth is nothing more than, as Randy Alcorn states in his work on *Heaven*, "a running head start into eternity." I love that!

I enjoy God in my way. You enjoy Him in yours. Just as we are unique children of God, He connects with each of his kids uniquely. I think of my sons James, Darby, and Colton. They are each wonderful in their own way and I celebrate that in them. I connect with each according to his specific bent and love them according to the language they connect with the most. I enjoy their uniqueness. How boring would it be to interact the same way with all people? I'll pass.

Tying it all up in a Christmas bow, you are alive during this time in history, in your geographical location to be radically sold out to your King, letting Him use you at any time, in any place, at any cost in order to draw the world closer to Him.

Sex Reciprocation

Let's use sex to embellish upon this thought.

Gary Chapman wrote a monumental book called the *5 Love Languages* that has sold over 13 million copies in the English language to date. Shanna's primary Love Language is Physical Touch. Weeknights will often find us on the couch watching a show while I rub her feet until she falls asleep. I love doing this for her and offer it freely. She absolutely loves massages and will do anything for them. Anything.

Early on in our marriage I discovered this truth and—in my immaturity—exploited it. We had an unspoken rule of reciprocation that said, "If I give you a back massage or foot rub you will reciprocate by giving me sex." Sometimes I'd start rubbing her shoulders, like the great husband I am (ha ha) and she'd say, "Honey, I don't want to make love right now", often accompanied by my childish whining. I'm ashamed and embarrassed to admit it now. My expression of love was simply a manipulative, childish, way to exploit my wife's Love Language and fulfill my carnal desire for sex.

But sex, for us now, is rarely associated with massages like in the earlier years. I rub her feet or massage her back several nights a week without her requesting it, and without whining for her to make love to me. I always, almost always, say yes when she wants a massage of any kind. Truth be told, I'm not sure who enjoys her foot rubs more, me or her. I know how much she loves being massaged and I know how much I love her. Pleasing her through service is a win-win for both of us. I love serving her and she loves getting massages.

The sex? Oh yeah, I thought you might ask. I don't have to beg, massage, or do the dishes ahead of time (although doing dishes certainly helps). She makes love to me whenever I want because she loves me, loves to love me, and serving me blesses her. It's a win-win-win-win!

"We love, because He first loved us" (1 John 4:19).

I am sold out to God because Jesus was sold out for me. Even my desire to serve God was instigated by the conviction of the Holy Spirit within me. We can't boast about how much we serve God, passionately pursue Him, or the magnitude of how He uses us, because it all comes back to Him and His great love for us! We take pleasure in pursuing God because He first chased us by showing His love for us by dying (Romans 5:8)!

Love God. Then What?

God did not create you, place you on this planet during this time of history, in this geographical place because you "need" to overindulge with more stuff—like many soft American males today. He placed you here because you need God and the world needs your help in discovering Him as Lord of their lives. The world is desperate for authentic men who thrive at being the best versions of themselves.

One of the most often quoted sayings in the Church, not from Scripture, dates back to St. Augustine of Hippo (354-430 AD). St. Augustine is the most published author ever in Christendom with over 150 published works to his credit! However, this beloved quote came from a sermon and not a book.

"Love God and do as you please."

Or, "Love God and do as you wish."

Or, "Love God and do what you will."

Pick the version you like most and go for it!

If Augustine had read Warren's, *The Purpose Driven Life* I bet he would have said, "Love God and live according to your SHAPE." That's my interpretation and I'm sticking to it!

No kidding!

In the midst of being sinful, God calls us saints. We aren't perfect but we can love God perfectly. Before you get bent theologically out of shape, let me tell you about my everyday carry knife. It stays clipped into my left pant pocket. It's scratched. The tip is slightly bent. The clip bolts have been glued in. The blade is dirty. But it's sharp—razor sharp. Beat up, flawed, and scratched, it does what it was created to do. It cuts!

Men are the same way. In three of the four Gospels Jesus admonished his followers to love God with everything they have. I believe it's possible. I've seen it time and time again. In the midst of your flaws, scars and sin, when you love God with everything you have, you become free to chase your heart's desires, and God will be pleased with the pursuit.

Augustine's statement, "Do as you wish" is contingent upon you being radically sold out for Him. Your will comes into alignment with His will when you love God with all your heart, mind, soul, and strength—with everything you have.

Stay in Your Lanes

Two times in this book we explained that the Greek word **dioko** was used either as a hunting word describing the pursuit of game, or as a track and field word meaning "to chase."

All three of our sons ran track in high school. We were compelled to stay to the end of every meet because each ran the last event—the long anticipated 4 x 400 relay. Each team has four runners who individually race once around a 400-meter track. To make the race effective and fair the runners are staggered, each in their respective lanes, and must stay in their designated lane for the first lap only, then the remaining three teammates can run on the inside lane.

The 4 x 400 reminds me of *Proverbs 3:5-6: Trust in the Lord with all your heart and lean not on your own understanding; in all your ways submit to him, and he will make your paths straight.*

Trust God and stay in your lanes! As mentioned earlier in this chapter, we're created to pursue God but each pursues Him according to our bent or lane. There are many ways to chase after God and I want to guard you from the guilt of trying to pursue God like someone you admire and want to emulate. Discover your own rhythms and methods of pursuit!

What lane will you use in your passionate pursuit of God?

Pursue God in the way that fits you! As a Christian man, paid to be a pastoral type, may I humbly present to you some lanes I've used to chase after God.

Power Source. Recognize that God gives power through His Holy Spirit to enable us to pursue God and to give us the passion we need. This supernatural empowerment does not work independently of the other lanes that follow. Galatians 5:25 says, *"Since we live by the Spirit, let us keep in step with the Spirit" (NIV).* Tune in to what the Holy Spirit is saying and doing, then walk in obedience to His leading.

Bible Study. I firmly believe a man should know the Word better than anyone in his household. How you do that is up to you. Listen to Bible teachers on the radio or favorite podcast station. Listen to the audible Bible through a Bible app. Read the Bible on your own. Sit under a Bible teaching pastor. Study one of our many resources for men (www.meninthearena.org) with some buddies.

.   .   .

Brotherhood. The strength of our organization, Men in the Arena, comes from the brotherhood developed when men share life together. Find a group of men to meet with weekly and lock arms with them in Christian fellowship. Pursuing God with godly men is transformative.

Christian Service. Find an area to serve God and serve people. Men in the Arena team leaders consistently report that they grow more by leading a team then by being a participant. Join our Men in the Arena closed Facebook forum and ask about becoming a Local or Virtual Team Captain.

Worship through music. I enjoy worship music on a weekly basis. Shanna connects the most with God through worship music. This may be a great lane for you as you drive to work each morning.

Prayer. Don't push me off the track, guys. I know how limited we are with our daily production of words. Hear me out. Let me knock the prayer chip off your shoulder. God gave you two ears and one mouth for a reason. Shut up and listen to what He has to say. Don't get wrapped up in talking to God. That's only a fraction of prayer. Prayer isn't **talking** to God as much as it's **tuning** in to Him. The following seven ingredients all go to creating a powerful prayer life.

Silence and Solitude. I love going to a dark room, waking up in the early morning darkness, and/or removing all stimuli so I can focus on God in a quiet place. Maybe that place is on your way to work with no radio or distractions, quiet prayer walks at lunch, or kneeling at your bedside before going to sleep.

Reflection and Meditation. I connect deeply with God in the mountains, next to a high mountain lake, or anywhere in nature where I can ponder God's wonderful creations and enjoy all it entails. I love reflecting on God through the beauty who sleeps next to me, or the sons that reflect my image, or the change in seasons. Men are made for reflection and meditation. Every good idea I've ever had was conceived in silence, solitude, reflection, or meditation.

Listen. Let's follow the example Jesus set of listening to His Father. With two ears and one mouth we should speak half as much as we listen! Take time to listen to God more than you speak to Him. That would drive a woman crazy but for us men it's incredibly freeing to know that we should listen more than speak.

Notepad. Whether it's a yellow note pad, notes app on my phone, or the top of my hand, I always carry on my person something to write down what I hear before I forget it—especially at my age, my friends!

Petition. Yes, I talk to God and ask him for stuff. I've used the Lord's Prayer (Matthew 6:9-13 and Luke 11:1-4) as an outline for decades. I've written an essay about the Lord's Prayer that I'll send to you if you'd like. Just message me and we'll shoot it over to you.

Homage. I do this in the Lord's Prayer but deeply desire to live a life of homage to God through living a holy life, praising God for **who He is**, and thanking Him for **what He does.**

Fasting. I go without food and sugary drinks for extended periods of time on a fairly regular basis. I've fasted for anywhere from 24 hours up to seven days. I know several people who have fasted for forty days but I'm not that hardcore! When fasting I highly recommend having a subject that you're fasting for. The main purpose of fasting is to connect with God and receive deeper revelation about your area of focus. If your motive is to lose weight, then it's not fasting but a cleansing.

Other books I highly recommend on this topic are Gary Thomas' *Sacred Pathways*, Richard Foster's *Celebration of Discipline*, everything by E.M Bounds, A.W. Tozer's *The Pursuit of God*, and James Bryan Smith's, *Good and Beautiful God.*

Strengthen Your Grip
Small Group Exercise

Rick Warren sold 35 million copies of his book, *Purpose Driven Life.* The book is summed up in his statement, "It's not about you. The purpose of your life is far greater than your own personal fulfillment, your peace of mind, or even your happiness. It's far greater than your family, your career, or even your wildest dreams and ambitions. If you want to know why you were placed on this planet, you must begin with God. You were born by his purpose and for his purpose." Why are you here? What did God mean when he created you? What is the purpose behind your life?

Proverbs 3:5-6 says, "Trust in the Lord with all your heart and lean not on your own understanding; in all your ways submit to him, and he will make your paths straight." What paths does God have you on right now? What alternate paths have you taken and where did they lead you?

What are your thoughts on Jim's statement that, "What you do does not define who you are! Rather, who you are should define what you do! How might your career be hindering God's mission for you during this season?

One of the most often quoted sayings in the Church that is not from Scripture dates back to St. Augustine of Hippo (354-430 AD); "Love God and do as you please." What does this mean to you? What must be in place in your life before you "do as you please?"

INTO THIN AIR
Walking with God

"I'd rather be fishing in the mountains and thinking about God than sitting in
church thinking about fishing."
~Unknown

Then Enoch walked with God three hundred years after he became the father of
Methuselah, and he had other sons and daughters. So all the days of Enoch were
three hundred and sixty-five years. Enoch walked with God; and he was not, for
God took him.
~Genesis 5:22-24

"I have been driven many times upon my knees by the overwhelming conviction
that I had nowhere else to go."
~Abraham Lincoln

Franchise Christianity

Years ago, I was sitting at a wedding reception table with some 20-something friends and a local pastor who had recently left his church to launch a radio ministry and had become an outspoken opponent of all local churches, calling them "Franchise Christianity." His crusade against the local church soon erupted at our peaceful gathering.

We politely listened to his rant but after some time I realized this guy wasn't going away any time soon, and I couldn't remain silent any longer. I jumped into the fray and a not so small "discussion" ensued. He got so frustrated at my Biblical defense of the local church, an evil in his opinion, that he angrily stood up, turned his back in defiance, and never returned!

I clearly got him thinking. But his radical views got me thinking too. Do I really need to be involved in a local church to follow Jesus? What's the point of the local church? Is God blessing it as a tool or is He cursing it as "Franchise Christianity"? Mostly, what does a Christian look like and how does he live?

After a heartfelt search I concluded that, yes, followers of Jesus **need** the local church, and God continues to use and bless local churches all around the world, even with their many flaws. More so, I identified seven habits that followers of Jesus practice whether inside or outside the local church. These are seven things that I believe are vital components to a dynamic follower of Jesus.

In Genesis we read about an obscure and mysterious man in the Bible named Enoch. As quickly as he appears in Scripture he vanishes—literally! His unique relationship with God is found in Chapter 5:22-24: *"Then Enoch walked with God three hundred years after he became the father of Methuselah, and he had other sons and daughters. So all the days of Enoch were three hundred and sixty-five years. Enoch walked with God;* **and he was not***, for God took him."*

God "took him"? Enoch and Elijah (2 Kings 2:11-12) are the only two men found in Scripture who never died. Even Jesus died before resurrecting. What does "walked with God" mean? What does it look like? What do people who walk with God actually do? Enoch didn't have a local church to call his home. He never owned a Bible. The Holy Spirit, as far as we can tell, had not been imparted to him. He didn't have Christian radio to listen to, or great podcasts to help him understand God. Yet he "walked with God" nonetheless.

Here's a simple acrostic to help you remember seven steps of walking with God using "walking" as our acrostic. Memorize and apply it to the spiritual rhythms of your life. Make **walking** with God one of your daily values and watch your life change! As we move through the seven steps notice the progressive verb tense. Walking with God is not a one-time event but daily habits, compounded over time.

Worshipping God Regularly

My favorite message about worship is subtitled, "Why dogs are better than cats." There are a million reason why but let me tell you a personal story that may be too gross for some of you to handle. Now I know you'll read on!

A while back I had an ingrown toenail that ultimately required surgery. It hurt to walk on and was full of pus, so I longed to take my shoes off at the end of the day for some relief. It oozed with yellow pus that would stick to my socks and send a twinge up my spine when I pulled my socks off. I actually cut parts of my toenail off just to experience relief. Nothing worked.

But the moment my shoes were off, my Yellow Labrador Ruger, would sense my pain and begin licking my infected toe! No joke. The cat would bolt out the door! The bottom line: dogs are better than cats. Think about it. When you treat a dog with love it worships you as god, but when you do the same for the cat, it expects you to worship it as god!

What's your point?

There are 11 words for worship in the New Testament but the Greek word **Proskuneo** (pros-koo-neh'-o) is mentioned more times than all 10 other words combined! According to the *Strong's Exhaustive Concordance of the Bible* the **proskuneo** of God is to, "prostrate oneself in homage (do reverence to—adore) ...kiss, like a dog licking his master's hand."

Look it up. It's right there. You can't make this up.

Where do you go to worship your God? Where do you go to sit at his feet (no licking in church please)? Worship is more than music, but it is one way I know to express our deep devotion to the Savior. I not only worship God with my life but regularly block time to **express** my worship (bow, raise my hands, clap, stand, sit, kneel, or lie prostrate) through music. As a non-musically gifted man I find my local church the best resource I have to worship my God. Yes, I can worship through music at home, in my car, or in the wilderness but the church has been an invaluable tool for regular worship. I do so only as authentic *proskuneo* to my God!

Approaching God Through Scheduled Blocks of Prayer

I'm tired of people quoting a solitary Bible verse, *"pray without ceasing"* (1 Thessalonians 5:17), as an excuse for a weak prayer life. Strong men pray. Reformer, abolitionist, and statesman Frederick Douglass once said, "I prayed for twenty years but received no answer until I prayed with my legs."

I have found that men function better when time is blocked out for prayer. Unceasing prayer is very difficult for our compartmentalized lives, especially for those men living in the Stress Bubble. Unceasing prayer is a high and lofty goal but unless you live under a rock it's simply not realistic for most of us. I love what Youth Specialties founder Mike Yaconelli once said to me, "I'm not great at prayer. I just think about Jesus all the time." Maybe he was closer to unceasing prayer than I thought at the time.

I remain, however, a firm proponent of blocking times to pray. Notice what Hebrews 4:16 says, *"Let us then* **approach** *the throne of grace with confidence, so that we may receive mercy and find grace to help us in our time of need."* To approach something requires timing and awareness, not unceasing autonomic response like breathing, digestion, or heart pumping.

In fact, Jesus himself set the example of prayer, sneaking away from the crowds regularly to do so. He had specific times he'd pray (Mark 1:35, 14:32, Luke 5:16, and 11:1). Before teaching his Disciples how to pray the Lord's Prayer (Matthew 6:9-13), he encouraged them to find a time and place for prayer: *"But you, when you pray, go into your inner room, close your door and pray to your Father who is in secret, and your Father who sees what is done in secret will reward you" (Matthew 6:6).*

Loving Other Christians Through Regular Fellowship

The night before Jesus' crucifixion is epic. The study of it changed my life and perspective of Jesus. Let's go back 2000 years and hide in the corner of the dusty upper room. Can you see the candles placed strategically? Do you see the thirteen pairs of sandals airing out on the floor? Can you smell the musk of a dozen men behind closed doors after the heat of the day? Do you see the basin filled with dirty water? Do you see the dirty towels Jesus used on the Disciples' feet piled in the corner?

Oh, only to be in that room on that night! Can you imagine the tension? Jesus, fighting back the anxiety, knowing it was his last moments before a gruesome death. Judas, anxious, knowing what he was about to do. Peter, clueless that he was moments away from the biggest failure of his life. Can you imagine washing the feet of your betrayer moments before the betrayal?

Knowing this really makes John 13:15 come to life, *"I have given you an example to follow."*

A few verses later, probably minutes, Jesus restated what he'd just modeled, *"A new commandment I give to you, that you love one another, even as I have loved you, that you also love one another. By* **this** *all men will know that you are My disciples,* **if** *you have love for one another" (John 13:34-35).*

The church is simply God's people. God designed the church for us to love and take care of each other. Over a lifetime of ministry, I've noticed an alarming trend—the first thing that stops when someone walks away from the things of God is fellowship with other believers (Hebrews 10:23-25). Men in the Arena teams are the perfect model for weekly fellowship with other men. If you are in need of fellowship, consider joining one of our Local or Virtual Teams. Frankly, we don't care whose group you affiliate with as long as you are becoming your best version in Christ, and that doesn't happen alone.

Knowing the Word of God

A few pages back I shared my conviction that a man should know the Bible better than anyone in his household. Let that resonate with you for a bit more. In their book *No Man Left Behind*, Morley, Delk, and Clemmer write, "We can say with confidence that we have never known a man whose life has changed in any significant way apart from regular study of God's Word."

How can a man wash his wife with the Word of God (Ephesians 5:25-26) if he's weak about what the Word of God says? It's time to rise up and speak out against Jell-O Jesus teachers who offer their "grace doctrine" as a license to sin. We desperately need strong men of the Word more than ever before who can reject such garbage! While writing this section I read of a megachurch pastor in New York who, when asked about abortion on a popular morning show, offered his Jell-O Jesus answer that, "Abortion is a matter of personal conviction."

I call BS! It's a matter of doing what the Bible teaches. It's a matter of murder.

Paul wrote to his pastoral protégé Timothy, *"Be diligent to present yourself approved to God as a workman who does not need to be ashamed, accurately handling the word of truth" (2 Timothy 2:15).* The Greek word translated "accurately handling" is **orthotoméō**, which means cut it straight. It's a picture of a man correctly swinging an axe or sawing a straight line on a piece of wood. If you've ever tried to split a piece of wood without hitting it straight, you know what I'm talking about.

Make it a habit to read the Word regularly. If you commute to work, listen to the Bible. Attend a Bible teaching church, download a Bible App, subscribe to a Bible teaching podcast! Know the Bible. Know it better than anyone in your family!

Investing Fiscal and Physical Resources in God's Kingdom

When God has your wallet, God has your heart. One of my really good friends is a Prepper. In an undisclosed location he has enough food for over 100 people to live on for an entire year. When Coronavirus began to shut down businesses, and hospitals were desperate for PPE (Personal Protect Equipment) he sent thousands of masks, meals, and dollars to those in need. We were not part of that group, but within a week received two random packages that blessed us greatly. We inadvertently became recipients of his blessing. When I called to thank him, he shot back, "It's all God's. I have this stored up to help others, not help myself."

I don't know who was blessed more—us or him. You see, my friend understands giving better than most people I know. But we don't like to talk about money, do we? I was taught as a child to never ask how much a gift cost, how much a person made in their job, or what a certain debt payment was. Have you ever wondered why talking about money is taboo?

It's because it's the god of the American Dream. Money exposes the heart of man.

The far and away majority of church attenders won't give a nickel to support their church, but they'll be the first to offer pastoral critique. Most church budgets are carried by less than 20% of the people who give 80% of the dollars.

Like my buddy we need to realize a Biblical fact: your stuff isn't yours. It's on loan from the God who owns it all (Psalm 24). You're simply a steward of your time, talents, and resources, including your money. If you claim to follow Jesus, hold your stuff with an open hand not a clenched fist.

"Each one must do just as he has purposed in his heart, not grudgingly or under compulsion, for God loves a cheerful giver" (2 Corinthians 9:7).

It's not about you. It's not about your stuff. It's about your God and what you do with **His** stuff. Become the cheerful giver God desires.

Nurturing Friends and Family into Disciples

Nowhere did Jesus say to make decisions for Him. Nowhere did He say to go into millions of dollars of building debt, water down the gospel message, and count converts. It must sadden the heart of God to listen to people boast about their churches more than Jesus. We've trained people to become "invite-alists" instead of evangelists.

Jesus said, "Go therefore and make disciples of all the nations, baptizing them in the name of the Father and the Son and the Holy Spirit, teaching them to observe all that I commanded you; and lo, I am with you always, even to the end of the age" (Matthew 28:19-20).

Cognitive assent is not salvation. Just because I convince someone to agree with my view of Jesus and pray the "Sinner's Prayer" doesn't mean that person is "saved". It may. It may not. The more important question is, "What happens next?" How can we strategically disciple people after they "receive" Jesus? Sometimes the evangelical church is more concerned about the decisions than discipleship. In this, we've failed miserably.

Attendance is not salvation. Attending a church doesn't make you a follower of Jesus. It just means you have a driver's license. Try this fun experiment. Walk into your local Burger King, stand on a table and proclaim to all patrons, "I'm a Whopper with cheese! I'm a Whopper with cheese!" Let me know how long before you're politely asked to stop or escorted to the local Psych Ward for an evaluation.

Discipleship is about nurturing someone along in their journey with Jesus. Who are you nurturing into a deeper relationship with Jesus? What role are you having in the discipleship of your wife? What about your children? Who are you strategically encouraging to walk with God? Who are you mentoring to be obedient to Scripture? Men are desperate to lock arms with other men and grow spiritually. Men need to be equipped like no other time in history. Stop trying to win a debate or coerce a decision and start nurturing the discipleship journey.

Giving Your Life in God's Service

Years ago a younger man asked me to mentor him. He was the church custodian, but things weren't going well. He had a nasty habit for a janitor. For whatever reason, he refused to clean the toilets. If he would have read the job description first, he might have realized the toilet cleaning is a large part of custodial work. Ultimately, church leadership was forced to fire him, but he quickly found a job across town as a youth director.

He wasn't ready. The pastor called me as a reference, and I warned him that if a guy can't be the church janitor, he isn't fit to be the pastor. About six months into this position he was fired for moral infidelity. If you won't clean the toilets, you certainly won't be able to clean up the crap in the lives of people!

Conversely, I had a freshman in my youth group named Josh who was a brand-new believer but was from a non-Christian household. He had no idea what it meant to follow Jesus, so he showed up at the church whenever the doors were open, followed the youth staff around, and bombarded us with questions about God, church, and the Bible. He was incredibly inspiring and annoying at the same time.

One night I was trying to manage 150 screaming middle schoolers when Josh started tugging on my shirt in his usual, "Jim......Jim......Jim...Jim..." fashion.

Frustrated, I turned around and snapped, "Josh, I'm in the middle of youth group! What do you want?"

"Well...um...someone dropped a dookie (poop) on the boys' bathroom floor."

Thoughts immediately raced through my mind, "Dropped? Where did they pick it up in the first place? I hope the kid didn't have corn for dinner! Was it solid or diarrhea? Oh, gosh! Here we go again!"

Suddenly Josh interrupted my inner grumblings with, "I already cleaned it up. I just wanted to tell you because it was pretty gross!"

Would you hire him as your youth pastor? Me too!

The man who walks with God lives his life in service of the King. He fights to push back the darkness. He's willing to charge hell with a squirt gun. I've never met a godly man who wasn't a tremendous servant, because the two go hand and hand. He lives to hear his Savior's words, *"'Well done, good and faithful servant. You were faithful with a few things, I will put you in charge of many things; enter into the joy of your master" (Matthew 5:21).*

With great longing, I foresee the day when after scratching and clawing and fighting my way up the mountain of life I breathe my last breath and, exhausted, I reach out to the invisible summit only to feel a hand reaching out to me. As the dark hand pulls me off the ground, I see the nail scars and cry out with joy, "Is this who I think it is?"

He wraps his nail-scarred hands around me and pulls me up to eye level and says those words I've longed to hear my entire life: *"Well done, good and faithful servant" (Matthew 25:21—NIV).*

. . .

I already have my response. I've rehearsed it all my life. I'll quote Luke 17:10, where Jesus said, *"So you also, when you have done everything you were told to do, should say, 'We are unworthy servants; we have only done our duty'"(NIV).*

Enter the fight. Join the fray. Jump into the arena and serve God now!

When a Man Gets It

This section is strategically the longest chapter of the book. In our five-volume curriculum, *The Man Card Series*, book three is called *The Summit*. In it are 10 team meetings and 50 daily readings, all designed to help men pursue God. When a man gets it—everyone wins.

But what is the "It"? A woman recently asked Shanna if "It" was sex. I love the concept and there may be some truth in that, but the short answer is no, "it" is not sex. Sorry guys!

It is God.

When a man dedicates his life to pursuing the King of Kings, everything changes and everyone around him wins! When a man surrenders his life to passionately pursuing Christ, his integrity is strengthened. He begins to fight apathy and becomes assertive! He leads courageously and his loved ones follow. And he will ultimately finish strong where others finish wrong!

God must be pursued before all things.

Strengthen Your Grip
Small Group Exercise

Someone once said, "I'd rather be fishing in the mountains and thinking about God than sitting in church thinking about fishing." What is the truth in this statement? What is the lie?

In Genesis 5:22-24 we read of an obscure man named Enoch who, "Walked with God; and he was not, for God took him." What does it mean to walk with God? How do you do this on a regular basis? What spiritual discipline habits have you formed?

There are 11 words for worship in the New Testament but the Greek word *proskuneo* is mentioned more times than all 10 other words combined! Why is this word so powerful and how does it manifest in your life?

Review the seven steps to WALKING with God acrostic. Where are you strong? Where are you weak? What steps are you going to take to grow stronger in your faith?

PART IV

THE DESCENT: LEADING COURAGEOUSLY

NOSE OVER TOES
Leading Downhill

If the mother is the first to become a Christian in a household, there is a 17% probability that everyone in the household will follow. If the father is the first to become a Christian in a household, there is a 93% probability that everyone in the household will follow. Men matter to God's work and the work of the local church.
~*Baptist Press Survey (1997)*

"I've done nothing and for that I am ashamed."
~*Benjamin Martin: "The Patriot"*

If it is disagreeable in your sight to serve the Lord, choose for yourselves today whom you will serve: whether the gods which your fathers served which were beyond the River, or the gods of the Amorites in whose land you are living; but as for me and my house, we will serve the Lord.
~*Joshua 24:15*

On the Summit

We began our journey at the trailhead of **protecting integrity**, experienced the grueling ascent of **fighting apathy**, and celebrated atop the summit of pursuing **God passionately**. But there is a problem with men. Men are conquerors. Once the summit has been conquered, where is the next mountain to climb?

Not so fast.

We celebrate on the summit but we'd better force ourselves to concentrate on the most treacherous part of our trek, which is yet to come.

"What are you talking about?" you may be wondering. "The hard part is the climb, right?"

Yes, but the more *treacherous* part is when you're coming down the mountain. It's actually where injuries occur most often. At the summit we can be deceived into thinking that the rest of the journey is simply a lighthearted downhill saunter before we return to our drinks on ice, waiting for us in the truck. The descent is when we're most tempted to lean back, relax, and lose focus. Not as physically taxing, but it's the most dangerous part of the trek. We'd better focus all our concentration and alertness on the dangers.

For proof let's look at the planet's highest summit and the one that kills the most men—Mount Everest.

Death Zone

The book, *Into Thin Air*, is John Krakauer's autobiographical account of the deadliest season in the history of climbing Mount Everest. The recounting of his summit experience had my eyes riveted to each page. Beyond the terrors of this account, however, he peers deeply into the **myth** of the world's tallest mountain. What is it about Everest that has compelled so many people to throw caution to the wind, ignore the concerns of loved ones, and willingly subject themselves to such risk, hardship, and expense?

Did you know that most problems on Mount Everest actually occur on the descent? It's true. According to Science20.com: "Counter intuitively, most deaths occur on the descent, in the so-called Death Zone just above 26,247 feet (8000 meters)."

What! Are you sure?

Instead of wondering if this statistic is true, a better question is **why** is it true? Here's my opinion. When it comes to Everest, everything I read points to several things. Besides lack of fitness and altitude sickness (which can lead to high-altitude pulmonary edema or cerebral edema), Krakauer's book alluded to pride and inexperience as predominant factors.

Pride, combined with inexperience, compelled climbers to ignore the turnaround time needed to descend safely. They continued climbing too late into the day, willingly—knowingly—putting themselves in grave danger as the unpredictable afternoon storms rolled in.

And it's not just Everest—the same is often true on shorter, lower climbs, like the ones you make.

I love hiking. It's a regular part of my week. Every hike has one thing in common, a hill to climb. When descending, I force myself to focus on the descent. I'm in far more danger of twisting a knee, ankle, or falling on the descent than on the climb. There's relief on the summit— accomplishment. It's during those times that I'm most tempted to lean back, relax my attentiveness to footing, and hurry homeward. Leaning back is more comfortable on the knees but far more dangerous as your traction is limited to the back half of the boot. To fully engage the descent after the summit, you must walk with your nose over your toes, which places more weight on the knees but is much safer.

Descent Lies

I've seen this tragedy countless times after a man surrenders his life to Jesus Christ and reaches the summit of manhood. He pursues God, grows in his faith, then leans back. He relaxes. He pulls back. This usually happens when his children are still in the home. Instead of relentlessly pursuing God and leading his family in the process, he relaxes and defers his spiritual leadership to the church.

Following are some of the **lies** that, if believed, can easily lead to a man's demise as the spiritual leader of his household.

The church will take care of it. Way too often, a man entrusts most of the care of his children and marriage to the local church, believing the lie that it's the church's job to disciple his family. It is not. He hands off the discipleship of his sons to a female-dominated children's ministry. With public elementary schools already dominated by female teachers, he entrusts even more females to do the spiritual disciplining of his sons (and daughters) while he sits in the bleachers observing passively!

He entrusts the spiritual care of his wife to the teaching of a pastor who in many cases can barely lead his church, let alone his family, and your wife! This is an incredibly unfair, spiritually immature, and Biblically lazy paradigm. Your children's ministry workers, youth staff, or the adult pastoral team have enough worries of their own without having your job dumped on them!

Do as I say not as I do. As a youth pastor for more than two decades I saw weaker churchmen, though well versed in the Word, climb out of the arena and take their seats in the anonymous bleachers.

They get burned out. They get wounded. They are tired from their many responsibilities before ever setting foot in the church. By the time my sons became teenagers and wanted more intentional involvement I was, in all honesty, tired. My parenting became less engaged as I went from my oldest to my youngest. The reason? I was tired, and dealing with teenagers seemed, well, difficult! And I was a youth pastor! Deferring leadership would have been the easiest thing to do. But it would have been the wrong thing. It's one thing to know the answers but it's another to be the leader.

I don't need the local church. Several men have excitedly shared, "This Bible study is my church!" My response to these and others like them is, "What about your kids? Who's fulfilling the work of the church to them?"

Crickets.

On our annual "Man Weekend" with my sons, the topic of church attendance came up. My job as a pastor mandated that my family attend church. From the day they were born until they left for college, my sons were in church every time the doors opened. We actually lived in one church's parsonage for nearly a decade of that time. Thankfully, they had two very positive church experiences, but were processing with me the years they were "forced" to go to church. During our discussion I simply shared that I have yet to meet a solid Christian man who was not involved in some kind of regular church gathering. Even with her many flaws, we need the local church that God continues to bless.

Even if you thrive in a men's small group without committing to a local body, it's your wife and children who will suffer the most when the local church is neglected. You are called by God to lead them to a local church gathering of some kind.

That's my wife's job. I work during the week and take weekends off. Let me get this right. It's your wife's job to disciple your children **and** teach your sons how to be men? It's your wife's job to affirm your daughters into beautiful women who are strong, confident, and worthy to be pursued? It's your wife's job to get all the kids ready and take them to church while you watch football all Sunday? Only a weak man would ever think that way. Strong men lead the way. The wife of one of our Men in the Arena recently shared, "My daughters finally have a father to measure every man against." Wow! That's a huge statement of a strong man who is willing to take the lead and be an example.

But there is another lie that creates more confusion than all other lies. Here it is.

I'm the Leader of My Home

This may come as a shock to you. Read the next sentence slowly. You are not the leader of your home. You read that right. The most mistaken sentence I hear from well-intentioned men is, "I'm supposed to be the leader in my home." In reality they know this isn't true but feel it's the right thing to say. It isn't. It's wrong. Christian men who flippantly use the phrase "leader in the home" need to reconsider the message this conveys to a man who tries to live by what the Bible says.

Let me explain.

If I were **truly** the "leader in my home", I'd live in a cabin or simple place somewhere in the mountains of Eastern Oregon. I'd have land that bordered government property, access to a natural water source, and be as far away from the city as possible. I'd use paper plates instead of ceramic, clean up when clothes needed washing, and never put the toilet seat down. I wouldn't own bed sheets or even know what a **duvet** cover is (I had to Google it just to spell it correctly)!

I'd be a barbarian. I'd be a savage. And I was. Thank God Shanna runs my home, and you should thank God your wife probably runs yours.

As witnessed by 300 people, on August 1, 1992, I read my vows to Shanna, friends and family. Since I was a barbarian, she'd only marry me if I vowed publicly to, "Do the best I can to pick up after myself around the home." No kidding. We still have our framed vows in the house. It was her idea. On that August day I read those vows with joy, because I'd have done anything to marry Shanna.

That meant the toilet bowl could no longer be my dog's drinking bowl. But it's cold and fresh, when flushed! I had to buy (and use) soap for the dishes. I had to pick up after myself. And I had to buy a vacuum—and use it. I had to throw out my dirty sleeping bag and start using clean sheets and blankets and, yep, a **duvet** cover. Sleeping with a beautiful woman was an awesome bonus.

Come on guys. Stop lying to everyone, boasting that you "wear the pants in your home". Sure, but she chooses the pants and what shirt to wear with them!

Before you burn this book, let me confess that I set you up. Your wife is most likely to be the queen of your castle, the home, but you rule the kingdom—the household. Make no mistake about it, you are the God-ordained leader of the **household**—your family—spiritually and otherwise. You'd better be too. Your wife and kids need you to be that man. They want you to be.

Nowhere in Scripture will you find men leading the inner workings of the physical home. They lead the household, the family. In the scholarly world Ephesians 5:22-6:9, Colossians 3:18-4:1, and 1 Peter 3:1-7 are known as the "Household Codes" where the Apostles Paul and Peter structured the leadership dynamics in Christian households, which included everyone from children, extended family, bondservants, and employees. The wife should offer and often initiate suggestions, advice, and discussion, but men have the final say in which direction to navigate the household. Men have the awesome responsibility to lead the family spiritually and otherwise.

In the Household Codes God wonderfully designed the family structure, removing all doubt from first generation believers about how the family unit functions. The man is the leader of the household, spiritually and otherwise.

But what does the leader of the household do?

Do something. Anything. Just lead!

In the movie, *The Patriot,* Mel Gibson's character, Benjamin Martin, mourns his lack of leadership after his family disintegrates, "I've done nothing and for that I am ashamed." How many empty nesters, reflecting back to the time when their children were in the home, lament their lack of leadership; "I've done nothing and for that I'm ashamed"?

When it comes to household leadership, do something, anything, just lead.

Strengthen Your Grip
Small Group Exercise

In this chapter Jim unpacks several lies men believe about spiritual leadership. Which lies have you bought into? Which lies have you exposed?

In Joshua 24:15 we read some of Joshua's last words in Scripture followed by his famous words, "But as for me and my house, we will serve the Lord." What are you doing to ensure that this will be true for your family? What are you doing to lead your family closer to the Lord?

In the movie, The Patriot, Benjamin Martin played by Mel Gibson reflects on his tragic losses and says, "I've done nothing and for that I am ashamed." How do his words act as a warning to you? What marriage and family regrets will you make sure are never experienced by those you love?

Brainstorm three new ways you can increase your spiritual leadership. What things can you do to lead those you love spiritually?

SPIRITUALLY CONFUSED LEADER
When in Doubt, Do Something!

For I, the Lord your God, am a jealous God, visiting the iniquity of the fathers on the children, on the third and the fourth generations of those who hate Me, but showing lovingkindness to thousands, to those who love Me and keep My commandments.
~Exodus 20:5-6

"It's harder to lead a family than to rule a nation."
~Chinese proverb

"A spiritual leader does not seek iconic status on his own but rather leans on God to provide wisdom and asks God to place men around him to be an example of a godly leader. A spiritual leader involves God in his decision-making and in day-to-day family life, from leading prayers at mealtime to involvement with community (church for example). A spiritual leader loves his wife as Christ loved the church (Ephesians 5) and leads his children by his example and not by relying upon secular institutions (like a public school) to do it for him. "No man is perfect at any of this. But the pursuit of God continues, despite failures and successes that should never deter us."
~Tom McFadden: Man in the Arena

Are You Talking About Me?

I remember running into a Christian mother and her teenage children at a local coffee shop. She was clearly the spiritual leader of her family. Making small talk, she asked about our organization, Men in the Arena, and I explained what we did for men and why. I explained our belief that when a man gets it—everyone wins.

Later that day I happened to run into the spiritually confused father of that family. When I recalled the conservation about men "getting it" as our organizational tagline, he got fried-egg eyes and shouted, "Wait! What? Were they talking about me?!"

I love that story and yes, they were.

. . .

Am I talking about you? Are you confused spiritually? Do you look at your pastor or other pillars in the church and get discouraged? Do you need direction? Do your children look to your wife for leadership? Are you anonymous in your church? Don't get discouraged. We've all been there.

You don't have to be the perfect spiritual leader; you just have to be good enough. Like my friend in the above story, you may be confused about spiritual leadership. That's okay. On some level we all are.

Any man who appears to have it all together is either faking or hasn't been watched closely enough.

If you've implemented what you learned in *Section Four*, you'll be in an elite category of men who follow Jesus, and your household will be better for it. Remember, when **you** get it—everyone wins! By far the most important thing you can do to lead your household spiritually is be an example as a follower of Jesus.

What about Me?

What about me? Don't ask me what I do because I probably do more than others, not because I'm some kind of spiritual giant but because all my life I've been a professional Christian—a pastor—paid to teach you how to do all things spiritual. I read the Bible daily, pray for hours on end, tithe on most of my earned income, serve hours on end, attend church daily, lead a large small group, have a model marriage, love the perfect wife, and raise flawless children, all of which are true!

Stop laughing. It's true!

Okay, you caught me. What a crock of horse dung I was slinging.

And no, in case you're wondering, I still won't tell you what I've done to lead my family spiritually. I have found that when professional (paid) Christians boast about their spiritual leadership it only serves to shame men who work in the secular marketplace. But I can offer some suggestions that I may, or may not, have done in the past to lead by spiritual example.

Okay. Okay. I'll tell you one story that you can steal and use with your family since I stole it from someone else of course.

Our family regularly vacations in Sunriver, Oregon. One night we went to a local Sports Grill to watch the Civil War game, which is a century-long rivalry football game between the University of Oregon Ducks and Oregon State

University Beavers. Our waitress attentively served us as we sat for several hours watching the game. After paying the $70.00 bill we gave her a 100% tip. We never saw her reaction to that tip, but my sons still reflect on that moment. To this day they bring up the "time we gave that waitress a 100% tip!" That moment of generosity was cemented in their memory.

You Are!

One day, a month before Christmas, the Men in the Arena team I led discussed ideas how to lead our families closer to Jesus at Christmas. The group was silent. Awkwardness ensued as the men stared back at me dumbfounded. Frustrated by their lack of response I asked, "What is a spiritual leader?" One guy, a tough prison guard and ex-college football player, glared at me and silently pointed his index (not middle) finger between my eyes.

"You are!" he exclaimed.

Heads nodded in agreement.

"Nope. You are!" I pointed back at his chest as if picking a fight.

For the first time, their eyes lit up. They got it.

Strong men don't **defer** spiritual leadership. They embrace it. They lean into it. Do you need some good ideas? Do you want to lead spiritually but don't know where to start? Google "spiritual leadership ideas". When I did it the page lit up with ways a man can be a spiritual leader.

Better yet, visit our website at www.meninthearena.org and you will be inundated with great ways to lead your family well, including the Men in the Arena Podcast, Facebook forum, blog and training videos. We even send a weekly equipping email to anyone who subscribes on our website. Finding ways to lead is easy. But leading is where the rubber meets the road.

You got this!

Brainstorm

I won't tell you what I do to lead spiritually not only because I am a paid Christian professional but because I may be further along in my spiritual journey than you. I may not be as well. But we can brainstorm ideas together. Besides Google, Men in the Arena resources, and asking older and stronger men you look up to, what else can you think of? Here are a few ideas to chew on.

Spiritual Leadership 101. Let's start with the painfully obvious elephant in the room. Visit a local church and take your family. The local church is the starting point for a strong man who desires to leverage his spiritual leadership capacity.

Other ideas are to pray with your family at meals. Attend a Christmas Eve and Easter Service. Start giving your resources (money) to those building God's Kingdom. Read your Bible. Serve others.

Spiritual Leadership 201. Attend a local church more than twice a month and take your family. Mandate (yes, require it) your children and teenagers to attend the youth group of their choosing. Find some way to serve in the local church. Annually read the Christmas and Easter story to the family. Get involved in a couples group with your wife. Read your Bible consistently. Pray over each family member before they go to bed. Read a verse a day at a family mealtime. Let them watch you tithe.

Spiritual Leadership 301. Include your kids in the giving process by letting them put your giving check in the offering. If you have children in the home **do not** give online but let them experience your giving firsthand. Lead a couple's group with your wife. Ask your children to pray over you before going to bed. Serve alongside your children in the local church. Read and study your Bible consistently and let your children "catch you" doing it. Leave your dust free Bible lying around the house as a mnemonic device that your family serves the Lord (Joshua 24:15). Tell them what you're learning.

Spiritual Leadership 401. Pray over others with your children. Regularly read and study the Bible with your family. Have them tell you what they're learning. Take your family on a mission trip and involve them in the process from fundraising to ministry. Annually have the children read the Christmas and Easter story to you. Mentor another couple with your wife.

Strong men and their families are different. Only God remains the same. You will connect your family to God differently than mine. That's okay. Find the lane that works for your family and stay in it. When in doubt make a choice. Do something, anything, just lead. A friend gave me some wise advice, "Sometimes wrong, never **in** doubt."

Lead decisively my friend.

Strengthen Your Grip
Small Group Exercise

What are your thoughts about the Chinese proverb that says, "It's harder to lead a family than to rule a nation?"

In this chapter Jim wrote, "You don't have to be the perfect spiritual leader; you just have to be good enough." What does "good enough" look like?

In Exodus 20:5-6 God says, "For I, the Lord your God, am a jealous God, visiting the iniquity of the fathers on the children, on the third and the fourth generations of those who hate Me, but showing loving kindness to thousands, to those who love Me and keep My commandments." This is one of the most often repeated sentences in the Bible! What generational iniquities (sins and bondages inherited from your parents and grandparents) are you breaking so that your children and grandchildren will be free? What "iniquity" will be passed on from you to your descendants unless you break free now?

Where can you improve as a spiritual leader? Where has your spiritual leadership not been "good enough?"

TIP OF THE SPEAR
Lead by Example

"Leaders are on point out in full view, each one becomes a target, and each one must anticipate being shot at."
~Marshall Shelley

Train up a child in the way he should go, even when he is old he will not depart from it.
~Proverbs 22:6

"You have to go out. You don't have to come back."
~Unofficial Coast Guard motto

Bring Them Back

Heraclitus (535–475 BC) is credited with one of my all-time favorite quotes. Also called the "Obscure" and the "Weeping Philosopher", he was a Greek philosopher from the city of Ephesus. He regarded himself as a self-taught pioneer of wisdom. Little is known about his life, and the one book he wrote, *On Nature*, is lost and only fragments remain today.

He believed the world was ultimately made of fire and was most famous for his insistence that things were in a constant state of flux or change as the characteristic feature of the world. This is recognized by his most famous saying, "No man ever steps in the same river twice."

This, however, is not my favorite quote from him. The first time I read my favorite Heraclitus quote was inside the Linfield College football locker room in McMinnville, Oregon, where my youngest son Colton was a four-year football starter. Dating back to 1956, Linfield boasts of the longest winning streak (65 as of 2020) in **all** divisions of college football! That's impressive. Tradition runs deep at Linfield and if you want to experience old school coaching and tradition, then Linfield is the place for you.

Here is the quote I've been hinting at:

"Out of every one hundred men, ten shouldn't even be there, eighty are just targets, nine are the real fighters, and we are lucky to have them, for they make the battle. Ah, but the one, one is a warrior, and he will bring the others back."

Strong men fully embrace that God designed them to be the **one**—the warrior —commissioned to bring his family back. The **one** who will lead the charge. The **one** who absorbs the impact. The **one** who willingly sacrifices his life. The **one** navigating for others. The **one** who cuts through all obstacles. The **one** leading by example, on full display. The **one** who braces for impact. The **one** who stays razor sharp. When that **one** gets it—everyone wins.

You're the man in the arena. You're the tip of the spear.

You Don't Have to Come Back

Disney's 2016 film, *The Finest Hours*, showcases the incredible bravery of four men of the Coast Guard. In life threatening conditions, Boatswain's Mate First Class Bernie Webber took his small craft out to a tanker called the Pendleton that had literally been ripped in half. They successfully rescued all but one of the ship's crewmembers who were adrift in the stern section of the vessel.

The four men thought they were on a suicide mission. The sea was battering the small craft with hurricane-force winds. Navigation systems smashed by raging seas, they miraculously located the wreck and picked up 32 crewmen, piling them into their small lifeboat. Webber and his crew then fought their way back into Chatham Harbor to an astonished group of onlookers who had given them up for dead. Webber was the **one** who brought the others back! What a story!

Stories of heroism like this are a regular part of the long history of the U.S. Coast Guard, which has the unofficial motto, "You have to go out. You don't have to come back." A strong man (contrary to a weaker male) is the tip of the spear. He is the one out in front, gladly willing to sacrifice his life for those he loves.

The antithesis to this is our media who loves to paint a deceptive picture of cowardly men. The media is a liar. Don't trust it. Just like fake news, the media produces fake reality, as entertainment, but not truth. It's like World Wrestling Entertainment (WWE). It's fun to watch but it's just a show.

Take the 1997 film *Titanic* for example, and its recounting of the tragic 1912 maiden voyage of the Titanic. In the movie, the lead actress is engaged to a cowardly millionaire who ultimately forces his way through women and children to steal a place on a lifeboat, ultimately costing a woman or child their life. But what the movie refuses to reveal is **the truth** about the brave men on the Titanic. Of the 2224 people aboard the Titanic that infamous night, only 710 survived. Of the 1514 people who died, 1347 were men!

Only 103 women perished in the tragedy, mostly because they were trapped in the lower decks.

Why?

Because men, strong men, brave men were willing to go down with the ship to save the lives of others.

You have to go out. You don't have to come back.

Men in the Arena

Being the tip of the spear requires certain things I've already mentioned. Writing this book, I surveyed the thousands of men on our closed Facebook group called Men in the Arena. This is a terrific resource for any man who wants to strengthen himself. It's there, men from around the world post and discuss questions, concerns and problems surrounding manhood. It's an exciting group to participate in. Recently I asked these men what it meant by the "tip of the spear" regarding spiritual leadership. Here's what some of them said:

It carries the burden of navigation. Bob Thomason wisely noted that the tip of the spear, "pierces through and penetrates to reach the targeted vital." Strong men lead the way and carry the burden of seeing the target within the big picture. They do more than talk—they act. Their purpose is to help those they love to become the best version of themselves.

It's in full view. It's on display. Man in the Arena AJ Miller responded, "It's leading by example. Plunging through life, leading my family to the target." As the tip of the spear, a man essentially says, "Watch me. Follow my example and I'll take you all the way." He isn't living anonymously but lives an authentic life, fighting to be the best version of himself for others. Kai Sorenson concurred with, "Lead from the front as an example for the rest to follow."

. . .

It absorbs the brunt of impact. I love what Man in the Arena Sam Roberts Jr. had to say, "It takes the brunt of the load. The tip of a spear is the first to hit the target absorbing all the opposing energy and transferring what is left to the rest of the spear. It focuses all the energy to a fine point. A sharp tip is the most important part of a spear, but it is also the weakest point. The tip of a knife or spear will break before any other part when it is used outside of its design." Spiritual leaders are willing to take it—to sacrifice themselves by absorbing the brunt of life in order to enhance the lives of others.

It is razor sharp for maximum impact. Abraham Lincoln is my seventh cousin and one of our great American presidents. He was definitely in the arena although he wasn't able to respond to our forum thread! He once said, "If you give me six hours to cut down a tree, I'll spend the first four sharpening the ax." So true. To be the most effective, a man must stay sharp at all times—stay focused.

It's the first point of contact. Man in the Arena Larry Dorrough said, "It's also a metaphor. I'm sure everyone's heard that phrase uttered by military personnel before an important mission. But it's true. They're the first, the tip of the spear. It's the same with our police and firemen and our first responders. They're the first on the scene. It's a phrase that defines leaders, a lead-by-example mantra that defines true leadership."

It is not an end to itself. Pastor, friend, and Man in the Arena Pete Hohmann offered great wisdom when he wrote, "The tip of the spear is the business end. The rest of the spear adds weight and stability. Without the shaft, the spear is either just a knife, or is only a little more effective than a rock. It will cut when wielded by the hand, but is more effective when it is thrust forward." That is so true! Men don't stand alone. They navigate the right path with other men who stand together with them. We're in this together.

It finds a way and makes a way. Man in the Arena, Dan Fleming wrote, "When it hits the mark it opens up the path for the others to follow through! It makes a way!"

Aren't those brilliant insights about the tip of the spear as a metaphor for spiritual leadership? The tip of the spear has to go out. It was made to be thrown, but the risk of being broken on impact is high. In the hand of a well-trained warrior it is a deadly force to be reckoned with. In the hand of a weak and untrained child it's only a dangerous toy. Aren't you glad your Master knows the way, shows the way, and has gone the way (1Peter 3:18)?

You have to go out. You don't have to come back. Do something, anything, just lead.

Strengthen Your Grip
Small Group Exercise

Heraclitus' words are worth repeating; "Out of every one-hundred men, ten shouldn't even be there, eighty are just targets, nine are the real fighters, and we are lucky to have them, for they make the battle. Ah, but the one, one is a warrior, and he will bring the others back." Regarding your family, where would you place yourself within the 100 and why? What does "bring the others back" mean to your family? What can you do to bring your family back"?

What are your thoughts on Marshall Shelley's quote, "Leaders are on point, out in full view. Each one becomes a target, and each one must anticipate being shot at."

Proverbs 22:6, "Train up a child in the way he should go, even when he is old he will not depart from it." Another way to translate the Hebrew "in the way that he should go" is, "according to his bent." How are each of your children different and how has that been reflected in your interactions with them?

How does being the spiritual leader and tip of the spear flesh out in your life? What qualities of leadership would your wife say you model best?

LEAD FROM THE BACK
Seeing the Big Picture

"It is well enough to tell people what we mean, but it is infinitely better to show them how to do it. People are looking for demonstration, not explanation."
~Robert E. Coleman: The Master Plan of Evangelism

"A leader is one who sees more than others see, who sees farther than others see, and who sees before others do."
~Leroy Eims

Hear, O Israel! The Lord is our God, the Lord is one! You shall love the Lord your God with all your heart and with all your soul and with all your might. These words, which I am commanding you today, shall be on your heart. You shall teach them diligently to your sons and shall talk of them when you sit in your house and when you walk by the way and when you lie down and when you rise up. You shall bind them as a sign on your hand and they shall be as frontals on your forehead. You shall write them on the doorposts of your house and on your gates.
~Deuteronomy 6:4-9

Tag Line Backfire

In 2012 we went all in with The Great Hunt for God with an exciting vision to "transform the lives of men." Since then much has changed. We changed our name to Men in the Arena. We changed our vision to include but not rely on "teams of men" for mission success. Our tag line changed to, "When a man gets it—everyone wins!"

If we only knew then what we know now we never would have chosen, "Lead from the back" as our original tagline. My first sign that this wasn't a great idea came from Shanna who got a strange look on her face and said, "That sounds kind of dirty, don't you think?"

I never thought of that. She was right. Unfortunately, the t-shirts had already been printed!

. . .

About a year later President Obama was using a similar phrase to explain his leadership style, which caused several men to question where I stood politically. This was problematic since I avoid political stances in ministry at all costs.

But I knew it was time to bury "lead from the back" when man after man needed an explanation. I'm a tip-of-the-spear kind of man and a tagline, which isn't necessary for organizational success, was causing men to question my convictions about reaching men with such a soft sounding tagline.

Reflecting on my leadership in those early years, I now realize that if the name of your organization, vision, or tag line is complex and needs constant explanation, you should kill it and move on. Again, I wish I knew then what I know now.

In everything from casual conversations to 30-second elevator speeches I found myself explaining our vision with, "because when a man gets it—everyone wins." It was simple. It was straightforward. It resonated with men.

Thus "lead from the back" was replaced with our current tagline.

This chapter explains our reasoning during those early days. I think you'll wholeheartedly agree with our original tagline, especially after I explain our brand—the arrow fletching.

The Arrow Fletching

I wouldn't label myself an archery hunter since I spend most of my hunting time looking through a riflescope. I'm more of an "archery opportunist" even though to date I've arrowed one buck, a couple of turkeys, and two trophy elk, thanks to the help of some friends. It takes countless hours of practice to make a "slam dunk" of a forty-yard shot. When preparing for an archery hunt, I'll shoot at least a dozen arrows, in groups of three, six or seven days a week, starting four months prior to a hunt. No joke. Archery hunters are serious about practice because they understand that all their time at the range, scouting in the field, purchasing equipment, and physical training all comes down to one shot; and it had better count! Prior to a hunt I'll remove my field tips and replace them with razor-sharp hunting tips—called broadheads. During this short window it's inevitable that I'll shoot the fletches off several arrows as the razor sharp broadhead blades slice through the target on impact. At the end of every arrow are three plastic veins, sometimes actual feathers. Together they are called a fletching. Individually they are known as fletches. If even one of the fletches are gone, the arrow will fly wildly every time until the fletching is replaced.

As we learned about spear tips in our previous chapter, the broadhead is the point of contact. But the broadhead is useless unless it is guided to the target by the arrow fletching. Ah! Now you're getting it. Without the fletching in the back of the arrow to guide, it will fly wildly through the air.

Imagine the fletching. What does each fletch represent when we're talking about men leading from the back? Let's take a look.

Fletch 1: Strategy

The fletching, along with the nock that locks the arrow to the bowstring, is just one in a three-part alliance that makes an arrow effective. The fletching navigates the arrow to its target. The arrow tip, or broadhead, is the cutting edge and first point of contact. The shaft of the arrow gives the arrow stability in flight, and it's weighted and cut to the length according to the archer's preference. It takes these three combined with the bow, bowstring, and a practiced archer to get the arrow to the bull's eye.

Leading from the back is strategically placing yourself in the rear to survey all that is happening. It means creating strategic alliances with your community, schools, church, and any entity that will take your family and marriage where it needs to go. You can't do this alone. It takes a village.

My son, Colton, shared another great observation about this. River guides are always positioned in the back of the boat. From there, they can navigate the approaching rapids, give commands, and make mid-stream corrections if the river demands it.

What about leadership? Coaches stay on the sidelines or high in the press box for a better view of the **big picture**. Generals never lead from the front lines, unless you're William Wallace in Braveheart. He died.

Rather they lead from a War Room or field command headquarters to direct the troops from a far and safe distance.

Both bull elk I've harvested were with my good friend Phil. Both times I followed him to the most strategic location where he positioned me in front of him and whispered instructions from the back. In 2006 I arrowed the "Web Bull". Full draw on the biggest animal I'd ever hunted, I whispered to Phil, who was on his knees behind me, "I'm shooting him with my 20-yard pin."

Behind me, rangefinder in hand, Phil whispered back, "I just ranged him at 42!"

I made the massive adjustment and today the Web Bull is proudly displayed in my home.

In this and the above situations, those in charge led from the back where they could see the big picture and offer winning instructions.

Men are the guides for **their** families. They position themselves to see what no one else sees, knowing that it's ultimately their responsibility to bring the others back, to navigate back down the mountain. Your wife may manage the day-to-day happenings of the home, but you're responsible for seeing the big picture of those within your household.

Every man on the *Men in the Arena Podcast* that we've asked about daily habits that help them become their best version, said virtually the same thing —**they take time every morning to think, reflect, read their Bible, and pray**.

Men are the tip of the spear, but they also lead from the back—they see the big picture. They strategically position themselves to see every possible contingency surrounding those they lead.

But leading from the back means something more.

Fletch 2: Sacrifice

Displayed in my office are several arrowheads I've found over the years. I have secret places I go sometimes just to look for them. When I'm in an area where natives once lived, I will set aside time to look specifically for shards (arrowhead fragments) and arrowheads. I celebrate every time I discover one of these long lost artifacts from men who survived in the wild.

But do you know what I have never done and never will? I will never look for an arrow fletching. Who cares about those? It's just a raggedy old feather anyway. The fletching never gets the credit.

The fletching is like an offensive lineman in football who sacrifices his body so the guys with the ball can get the glory. Have you ever seen an offensive lineman receive the Heisman Trophy as college football's greatest player? Me neither. Since the inception of the trophy in 1935 there have been exactly **zero**. But their sacrifices have been great.

Leading from the back takes sacrifice, which often goes unnoticed by the masses.

When I was a youth pastor in Los Osos, California, my wife and I led a Bible Study for a group of freshman girls. On one particular morning Shanna, 11 young ladies, and I dove into the household codes of Ephesians chapter five. The room angrily erupted when we read, *"Wives, submit yourselves to your own husbands as you do to the Lord" (NIV)*. These mostly unchurched, sweet, and godly girls quickly turned into ravenous animals, and I was the main course! My interpretation of "submit" calmed them down slightly but I knew the cards in my hand as I quickly moved to verse 25, *"Husbands, love your wives, just as Christ also loved the church and gave Himself up for her."*

Then I asked, "Ladies, the Bible asks you to have an **attitude** of submission —to willingly empower your husband to be the best version of a man by trusting (and demanding) that he leads you."

"But the Bible tells your future husband to die to his desires and sacrifice his life so that you can have yours. He is called to be Christ to you and lay down his life for you through the **action** of sacrifice. Could you submit to a man who willingly places your needs ahead of his, joyfully serves you, and gladly sacrifices his desires for your happiness and well-being? Could you love that kind of man?"

They physically melted into their chairs and sighed in unison, "Ahhhhh... Yes, we'd love that!"

I had them eating out of my hand, which was way better than eating my hand itself. I might survive this study after all!

The high call of strong men is the call to sacrifice. Weaker men defer sacrifice to some other man who is willing to take the hits that were meant for them. Just like my friend Phil knew the exact distance and how to best position me for the shot, the strong man surrenders himself to Christ and sacrifices his desires on behalf of those he loves.

Fletch 3: Service

I stated earlier that I became a man when I was 30 years old. I'd been a husband for years. I was a father. I was a pastor. I was a male. Prior to that, Shanna and I had a love-hate relationship. But we hated each other most of the time. Our marriage got so bad that I prayed on numerous occasions for God to "take her out" so I didn't have to divorce her and leave the ministry. That is sick on so many levels. I'm ashamed. But it is true.

That all changed one day in 1995 when I decided to out-love and out-serve my wife and have done so almost every day since. Today I'm blessed to sleep next to my best friend and most important person in my life. My desire to serve changed our marriage because when a man gets it—everyone wins. Males, weak men, serve themselves. Men, strong men, serve those they love.

Life is messy. Marriage is messy. Your job is messy. Your church is messy. Put on the servant towel of Jesus and start cleaning up the messes!

After a message I gave at a Men's Advance Weekend (they said "men never retreat"), a tough-looking man in his late 60s with a military flattop approached me, "I served my entire military career as a Gunnery Sergeant. Do you know what sergeant means in the Latin?"

I joked, "Unless it's in Pig Latin, I don't."

He didn't laugh. He was dead serious. I braced for impact, "It means servant."

He was absolutely right. According to vocabulary.com, "Sergeant comes from the Old French *sergent* and originally from the Latin verb *servire* meaning 'to serve,' as in 'to serve and protect,' a police sergeant's job."

I've never forgotten this. I never will.

Leaders get behind and serve. Strong men are serving men. Weak men are selfish men.

Hopefully you're convinced that a man leads from the back as well as being the tip of the spear. Like the fletching on an arrow he **strategizes** on behalf of those he loves and leads. He sees the big picture and locks arms with those who will assist him in navigating his family through life.

He **sacrifices** his life for those he leads. He lives like Jesus. He sacrifices his time, his resources, and his glory to put others on display. He surrenders his wants to help his wife and children become the best version of themselves.

Lastly, he **serves**. He's not afraid to get in the arena of life with its blood, sweat, and tears, so that he might bring joy to those under his charge. He's a strong man.

A Dangerous Prayer

Are you ready for a challenge? I know what you're thinking, "I've already been challenged enough. What else does this guy want from me?"

I want you to pray a dangerous prayer. For the next 30 days pray this, "Put me on display!"

That's right.

I've been praying the Lord's Prayer as my quiet time for decades. It's my go-to prayer. The crescendo is at the very end of the prayer when I ask God to put me on display for Him. Matthew 6:13, *"For Yours is the* **kingdom** *and the* **power** *and the* **glory** *forever. Amen."*

But it's there and I pray those powerful words regularly. Here is how I make a dangerous prayer even more so:

For Yours is the kingdom. Attend a local church. Get involved. The local church needs men to lead the way. The church's denomination is usually unimportant as long as the Bible is preached and people take following Jesus seriously. Only one denomination will be in Heaven, those men and women who followed Jesus. God's Kingdom is not just Heaven. Jesus taught us to pray that God's kingdom would come to us on earth **as it is** in Heaven. What, then, is it like in Heaven? Heaven is the place God dwells, and where his subjects obey Him perfectly. It's where God reigns unequivocally. His **rule and reign** over your life now is defined perfectly in *Matthew 6:10, "Your will be done on earth* **as it is** *in heaven."*

I will always be associated with a local church because I believe in her. But I am a sold out follower of Jesus Christ committed to God's Kingdom (rule and reign) at all costs.

And the power. I want God's power. More of it. All of it. I won't use it (God help me) to arrogantly build my own kingdom or for personal recognition. In humility, I want to wear the servant's towel and allow God to put me on display. This is only possible if He empowers me with the Holy Spirit to accomplish His will for me and endow me with power from on high. I desperately need to tap into the power of God's Holy Spirit, which empowers me to surrender to God's reign daily.

And the glory forever. Endowed with power, put on display, and building God's Kingdom, I vow to put God on display whenever man attempts to put me on display. I reject personal glory, deferring to the only One who is worthy of glory, and honor, and praise. I promise God that, to the best of my human capacity, I will point others to Him when they point to my frail achievements. I will reflect God's glory, then deflect any credit for victories I experience back to the One who used me mightily.

This is a dangerous prayer because it's a declaration that you will no longer be satisfied as an anonymous spectator. It's a dangerous declaration of you rejecting the anonymous bleachers to battle in the fray—the arena where only the strong men survive.

Theodore Roosevelt recognized the dichotomy between the two. The bleachers are safe, anonymous, and comfortable, but the man in the arena is easily recognizable as one,

> *"whose face is marred by dust and sweat and blood; who strives valiantly; who errs, and comes short again and again, because there is no effort without error and shortcoming; but who does actually strive to do the deeds; who knows the great enthusiasms, the great devotions; who spends himself in a worthy cause; who at the best knows in the end the triumph of high achievement, and who at the worst, if he fails, at least fails while daring greatly, so that his place shall never be with those cold and timid souls who know neither victory nor defeat."*

Get in the Arena

Lead courageously. When the weaker men surrounding you lean back and relax, choose to lean into your God and jump onto the arena floor. Get your nose over your toes and do something, anything, just lead.

Strengthen Your Grip
Small Group Exercise

What contrasts can you draw between being the tip of the spear and the arrow fletching that leads from the back? What paradox do you see? How does each contribute to spiritual leadership?

In the classic book on leadership, *The Master Plan of Evangelism*, Robert E. Coleman wrote, "It is well enough to tell people what we mean, but it is infinitely better to show them how to do it. People are looking for demonstration, not explanation." What are you positively modeling to those you love about following Jesus? And what are you negatively modeling, such that you need to make changes?

What does Leroy Eims' statement, "A leader is one who sees more than others see, who sees farther than others see, and who sees before others do," teach you about spiritual leadership?

Deuteronomy 6:4-9 says, "Hear, O Israel! The Lord is our God, the Lord is one! You shall love the Lord your God with all your heart and with all your soul and with all your might. These words, which I am commanding you today, shall be on your heart. You shall teach them diligently to your sons and shall talk of them when you sit in your house and when you walk by the way and when you lie down and when you rise up. You shall bind them as a sign on your hand and they shall be as frontals on your forehead. You shall write them on the doorposts of your house and on your gates." What insights help you to see the big picture for your family?

Theodore Roosevelt recognized the dichotomy between the man in the arena and the anonymous man in the bleachers when he said, "The credit belongs to the man who is actually in the arena, whose face is marred by dust and sweat and blood; who strives valiantly; who errs, and comes short again and again, because there is no effort without error and shortcoming; but who does actually strive to do the deeds; who knows the great enthusiasms, the great devotions; who spends himself in a worthy cause; who at the best knows in the end the triumph of high achievement, and who at the worst, if he fails, at least fails while daring greatly, so that his place shall never be with those cold and timid souls who know neither victory nor defeat." Where have you remained in the bleachers for too long?

PART V

THE END OF THE TRAIL: FINISHING STRONG

THE EMPTY GUN CASE
Finishing Wrong Vs. Finishing Strong

"In the Christian life, it's not how you start that matters. It's how you finish."
~ Steve Farrar: Finishing Strong

For which one of you, when he wants to build a tower, does not first sit down and calculate the cost to see if he has enough to complete it? Otherwise, when he has laid a foundation and is not able to finish, all who observe it begin to ridicule him, saying, "This man began to build and was not able to finish."
~Luke 14: 28-30

"You don't have to be the best. You simply have to outlast the rest."
~Life Motto

The Trail's End

I trained with a weighted backpack all summer to prepare for the high-country mule deer hunt with my son Darby in Oregon's Strawberry Wilderness. The day before we left Darby got the flu but decided to tough it out anyway, sleeping the entire five-hour drive to the trailhead. That young man is tough. It started snowing at the trailhead and by the time we packed in six miles and 3,000 grueling feet of vertical gain there was six inches of unexpected snow on the ground.

Our hike out, downhill, through the snow, took us over three hours before reaching the truck. Near the end of the trail, we searched around every corner hoping to see my elusive truck where we could enjoy a warm pot of Jet Boil coffee and a reconstituted dehydrated meal. I can't explain the relief it was to drop our packs, pull out some camp chairs, and sit down! I can still feel the frigid air piercing my sweat drenched back after setting my gun and pack on the ground.

Chip on the Shoulder

Like the joy of seeing my truck around the last bend, here we are in the last section of this book. I hope you're still tracking—fully engaged and expectant around each of our four final corners. I trust you've enjoyed reading this as much as I enjoyed writing it. Thank you again for taking the time. I'm humbled that you picked up *Strong Men Dangerous Times*, and promise the best is still to come. We are living in dangerous times and we need strong men like never before. If you're reading this, then you are a man on a journey to greater strength. For that, I salute you! You'll find the tone of this final section different from the others—because it's personal.

For the past twenty years I've read an average of two dozen books a year, plus the Bible, and have authored several books of my own. With our high caliber, world-changer guests on the Men in the Arena Podcast, I'm currently reading an exhausting 40-50 books a year. I give away or discard dozens of books a year and still maintain a library of more than 1000 books.

All that to say, I am well versed on the art of book reading and writing. In my experience most books start out strong and finish weak. Authors, like men, spend the early pages making their most powerful points then slowly fade to the Epilogue (Epitaph for men). Using Italian economist Vilfredo Pareto's (1848-1923), Pareto Principle as a guide, if you read the first 20% of a book you will usually get 80% of its best content. That's just an observation. Take it or leave it.

I think I'll write my next book from back to front.

The structure of this book doesn't allow for a weak ending. In fact, I promise to end with an exclamation mark!

Admittedly, of my five essentials every man must possess to change his world, "**finishing strong**" was birthed from life circumstances, observations, and raw pain. Where the previous four sections address what manhood is and does, this section addresses a chip I have on my shoulder. For example, I have been attending church regularly since 1989 and not a single man who served as my senior pastor retired as a senior pastor. Not one. Some had moral failures. Some simply burned out. Others opted for the secular work force where they could double or triple their income with substantially less head and heartache. Either way, they have faded into the murky waters of those who began with a passionate call from God and, for whatever reason, faded to gray.

. . .

Personally, I bear witness of the pain caused by men who finish wrong. December is a month that brings back some of those painful memories. My birthday is in December. Christmas is in December. December should be a month of fond memories, but it was on my birthday in 1978 my parents gave my brother, sister, and me the "It's Not Your Fault We're Getting a Divorce" speech. After fifteen years they threw in the towel and walked away from each other for good.

I love both my parents and am very close to each. Dad was the Best Man in my wedding. But their divorce hurt. It hurt deeply. It's healed now but I still have the emotional scars as a reminder to finish strong and fight to the bitter end.

December is also the month of a horrible family tragedy that left me with a permanent chip on my shoulder.

Finishing Wrong

A divorce is a finish to a covenanted relationship, but a wrong one. Getting fired from a job for reasons you could have prevented is a finish, but a wrong one. Walking out on your teammates midseason is also a finish, but a wrong one. I'm annoyed by the recent trend with college coaches who preach a never-quit attitude to their players yet take a more prestigious coaching position and walk away before the final game of the season—another wrong finish. Beating a team by a wide margin (or losing by a large margin) and throttling down to coast until the final whistle is another wrong finish. Scoreboards have little to do with finishing strong.

You're probably wondering about the chapter title, *The Empty Gun Case.* Let me share the finishing wrong story that I hinted at in the end of the last section. December is also the month our family acknowledges another painful anniversary. On December 21, 2012, my stepfather of over thirty years died tragically by his own hand.

We'll never know why it happened. His pain died with him on that day but continued through his loved ones. He left a note that offered no clues. He was my stepfather from early high school on. He was a good man. He was good to my mom. He was a good stepfather. Our home was always the cool place to be thanks to his laid-back attitude. I liked him a lot.

. . .

But in the morning on December 21, he ended his life using the Remington Model 700 chambered in .270 that we gave to him on Christmas many years earlier. One year later the gun was released from evidence at the Sheriff's Department, and I was commissioned by the family to sell it. It hadn't been cleaned. The weapon was simply picked up and placed in an evidence box. In handwriting on the box are the words, "Found next to the body."

Suicide is also a finish, a painful one, and a very wrong one.

I know. Years later, the box sat only three feet from me in my office, a constant reminder to finish strong where others have finished wrong.

Teleological

While reading Donald Miller's book on relationships, *Scary Close: Dropping the Act and Finding True Intimacy*, I ran across a word I'd never heard before. In the book, Don tells a story of a friend who said relationships are "**teleological**". Wikipedia describes this word as: "A reason or explanation for something in function of its end, purpose, or goal."

Don's friend described all relationships as "going somewhere…living and alive and moving and becoming something."

Everything we start is teleological, whether we know it or not. Every relationship is going somewhere. Every commitment we make has an end. Every task we take on has a finish.

Henry Cloud in *9 Things You Simply Must Do* admonishes readers to "Play the Movie."

In his popular book, *7 Habits of Highly Effective People*, Stephen Covey coaches readers to "See the end at the beginning."

We've all had wrong finishes. We've all thrown in the towel at some point in our lives. But if you want to be a strong man and finisher instead of a weak man and wrong finisher, it's vital to understand the teleological nature of our choices. They're heading in a certain direction. They're crafting us into a certain kind of man, or male, for that matter. In fact, life is nothing more than our choices compounded over time. Be careful before you jump into a commitment. Be careful to sow only that which you'll be proud to reap later on. Be aware of the path on which your choices are leading. Be warned about the ending you are creating for your life.

. . .

Set a course to finish what you start, strong instead of wrong.

I'm notorious for overcommitting myself. I jump into the fray without counting the cost. Sometimes I forget to pray first, and dive headlong into a problem. I confess it. Several times, I've had to resign, repent, return with my tail between my legs—so to speak—and my shotgun approach to life has hurt my focus and hindered my dreams. The problem with a jack-of-all-trades is that he's a master of none. Run at a pace that allows you to make a strong finish. Take on tasks that you can finish strong. Reflect on the teleological nature of your marriage, relationships with your children, and friendships. Where are they heading? Have a vision. Have a plan that will lead to a good end.

Rebound Effect

I played basketball from fourth grade through high school and was a varsity letterman for three years for a very bad program. We won 18 games as a freshman and that many combined over the next three years! We weren't very good. In fact, out of nearly 1000 students in our high school, only seven played varsity basketball my Junior year. Three specific games that year come to mind. In the first one, we started the game in a Stall Offense to prevent the future state runner-ups from scoring 100 points.

It didn't work. Our six-foot tall posts (yours truly being one of them) were no match against three of their starters who were over 6'5" tall!

Another game ended with me and another teammate fouling out near the end of the game, and with our seventh man ineligible due to grades we were forced to finish the game with four players on the court!

We lost. We lost a lot.

But in a Christmas tournament, I actually broke the tournament record with fifteen rebounds in a game. And yes, we still lost.

Rebounds matter, on the court and in life. Men are remembered by their ability to rebound after failure. It's not whether or not you will fail that matters most. We all fail. Look at the Bible. It's riddled with failure after failure. King David, the giant slayer, and "man after God's heart" (Acts 13:22) committed adultery, was a horrible father, and a murderer! But God called him a man after His heart because David always bounced back to God after his failures.

Failures don't define you. **Finishes do**. It's not how you start that matters. It's how you finish. You don't have to be the best. You simply have to outlast the rest.

Keep shooting. Keep crashing the boards.

Look at Michael Jordan, arguably the greatest NBA player of all time (and I'm a Lakers fan). He may be the most famous player acknowledged in the history of the sport—winning six NBA Championships, the MVP trophy five times, playing in a dozen All-Star games, and winning two Olympic gold medals.

In a famous ad campaign launched by Nike, Michael is quoted saying he lost almost 300 games (that's more games than many NBA players ever play in), missed over 9000 shots (more shots than an average NBA player even takes), and on 26 occasions was given the ball for the game winning shot—and missed. Jordan goes on to say that the reason he has succeeded boils down to using failure as motivation to shoot for success. Jordan's career shooting average was just below 50%, so every other shot, on average, was a miss!

But he is one of the greatest players in NBA history. You're made for greatness too. You're called to impact your world of influence. Crash the boards. Keep shooting. Keep rebounding until the ball goes in the bucket.

I love an anonymous poem that drives home my point, "You cannot go back and make a brand new start my friend, but anyone can start now and make a brand new end."

Crash the boards.

Strengthen Your Grip
Small Group Exercise

What is the difference between finishing each day strong versus wrong? In your life how do the two finishes look different in your day?

In his book, *Finishing Strong,* Steve Farrar wrote, "In the Christian life, it's not how you start that matters. It's how you finish." What is the danger when wrong finishes outnumber strong finishes over time? What kind of man, husband, and father are your daily finishes leading you toward?

In Luke 14: 28-30 Jesus warned, "For which one of you, when he wants to build a tower, does not first sit down and calculate the cost to see if he has enough to complete it? Otherwise, when he has laid a foundation and is not able to finish, all who observe it begin to ridicule him, saying, 'This man began to build and was not able to finish.'" What costs have you failed to count and how will you fix it?

Jim shared about his life motto that, "You don't have to be the best. You simply have to outlast the rest." Where is the truth in that for your marriage, parenting, and church?

QUITTERS NEVER WIN
You Don't Have to Be the Best...

"Never give in, never give in; never; never; never; never—in nothing great or small, large or petty—never give in except to convictions of honor and good sense."
~Winston Churchill

"I have fought the good fight, I have finished the course, I have kept the faith."
~Paul, the Apostle

"I'd made it this far and refused to give up because all my life I had always finished the race."
~Louis Zamperini

Life Change in the Locker Room

It was just one month after my parents gave us the Divorce Speech in January of 1979. I was hurting. I was wrestling with my parents' dating other people, the two separate Christmases, and life with Dad out of the house. To make matters more awkward, I was at Laguna Middle School getting ready to play against my old schoolmates and neighborhood buddies I used to hang out with prior to moving out of the neighborhood a few years earlier.

As our team mustered for pre-game warm up feet away from the basketball court, I saw it. Written across the coach's office window was a phrase that changed my life. That single quote has outlived them all. For years, that quote was proudly displayed on a plaque in my office. It is my war cry.

A quitter never wins.

A winner never quits.

In that locker room moment I knew I would fight to win in life. I would fight to win in marriage. Even if I wasn't good, even if I was beaten down, even if the odds were stacked against me, and even if I stood alone—I would stand, nonetheless. I would never quit, never throw in the towel, and never surrender.

. . .

That's why the words of Winston Churchill resonate so deeply, "Never give in, never give in; never; never; never; never—in nothing great or small, large or petty—never give in except to convictions of honor and good sense."

We live in a world of quitters.

Heck, quitting is expected. We even have "No Fault" divorces. Really? I have a better idea. Maybe we should charge divorcing couples a fine. Or better yet, pass a law that divorce is illegal except for extreme cases? Maybe then people would be forced to fight for their marriage instead of ending a marriage behind ambiguous—unbiblical—grounds like abuse, unfaithful, and addicted. I already hear the excuses. Win or die trying. Have some grit.

We need strong men of grit who are committed to finishing strong at all costs. We need strong men winning, not weak ones whining. The one difference between whiners and winners is that whiners want to feel good **before** they get to work, whereas winners work at something **first**, and feel good about it later. Which are you?

Moving on to Something Better

As a young man in my thirties I came to a crossroads between full-time coaching and ministry, and eventually opted for ministry. Football was a huge part of my life growing up and the catalyst God used in my spiritual awakening. To this day I think about what life would've been if I'd chosen to serve God through coaching over ministry. No regrets.

I have some great memories of the 20 years coaching football, and some not so great ones. Here's one I'm not proud of. It was a coaching failure I'll never forget. I'd taken over a freshman football program that had a 2-16 record after two seasons. In the two seasons following, with the help of some great assistants and tremendous athletes, we ended 13-4 overall.

My reputation was that I cared for the athletes, on and off the field, and that I was a hard but fair coach. I love to win and refuse to play favorites or discriminate based on ethnicity, demographic, or religion. Winning motivates me. I admit it. In our Participation Trophy world you may think, "Why care about who wins? It's your effort that matters."

Wrong.

I agree wholeheartedly with what Vince Lombardi once said, "If winning isn't important then why do they keep score?"

. . .

I was tough on our young men. Maybe too tough at times. I was strategically the toughest on my own sons, so no one could ever accuse them of being on the starting team just because their dad was the coach.

One young man in particular comes to mind. My tactics were too much for him and he quit. In my conversation with him I shared that quitting, even if you don't like the coach, is a problem that can hamstring a person in life. To cause any young man to quit is a failure on my part. I own that. Surprised by my humility, he accepted my apology and we parted ways. I did, however, acknowledge my failure as **his** coach and asked for forgiveness, which I could tell by his fried egg eyes had caught him off guard.

In fact, I received two phone calls that night; one from his livid dad, and the other from his irate mom. They had apparently not coordinated their attacks. In both conversations I explained my coaching style and my opinion about quitters. His dad calmed down but not his mother. The call ended with her sardonically saying, "Well, I guess I'm not a man, so I don't understand."

I enthusiastically agreed with her. That didn't help the situation.

Obviously dissatisfied with the conversation, she showed up at practice the next day to make her point even clearer, but in her rant she said something I'll never forget.

"My son **is not** quitting! He's moving on to something better!"

I calmly rebutted her flawed logic saying, "Using this excuse in high school sports is no different than telling your children, 'I'm not quitting the marriage. I'm just moving on to someone better.'"

Her eyes lit up like I was reading her mind. We agreed to disagree and parted ways.

A short time later, she divorced her husband and moved on to someone better.

Let's call it what it is. It's quitting. It's finishing wrong.

Retirement and Entitlement

Youth soccer is similar to rugby in one way. Two teams form a large amoeba and move in unison up and down the field until one ingenious boy or girl decides to step outside the amalgamation to take a shot on goal, which is unattended since the goalie is wither in the scrum with the rest or building a bouquet of dandelions!

When my youngest son, Colton, was a child playing co-ed soccer, it was no different. Recreation soccer stipulated that no team kept score (we did it anyway), there were no winners (or losers), and be kind to the teenage referees who were trying to make a few dollars after school. I didn't coach because I couldn't reconcile coaching a sport where there are no winners and using your hands is somehow forbidden. To all my soccer loving friends, please forgive my jesting. I did, however, attend every game to encourage Colton to play outside the amoeba and score, which to my joy he did often.

We had so much fun cheering on the amoeba that one parent had trophies made for everyone on the Kelly Green Team (teams were named by color). Did the children demand a trophy for playing on a team their parents funded? Did the children demand that we not keep score to prevent hurt feelings? Was the trophy earned? Was there a season champion that exceeded the others?

No.

The parents did that. We are to blame. This generation will be held in infamy for our invention of the Participation Trophy. My generation of parents have been tagged with alarming labels such as Bulldozer and Lawn Mower parents who knock down every obstacle in entitled little junior's path on the way to him becoming a spoiled weakling. Unlike the Helicopter Mom or Dad who hover over their child, the Bulldozer/Lawn Mower Parent removes all obstacles from their child's way. They clear the path for their son or daughter's perceived success. They remove responsibility for their child's actions by wordsmithing their kid's mistakes and poor decisions to sound better than they are, "He's not quitting. He's moving on to something better."

They receive a Participation Trophy, win or lose. If I can protect little Johnny from harm's way, he'll be free to grow up as a healthy, well-adjusted man with a strong sense of self-esteem.

Wrong.

Little Johnny will grow up to be an entitled, spoiled, maladjusted male who refuses to accept responsibility for his actions!

I was tailgating before one of Colton's Linfield College football games and started a conversation with what seemed like a committed parent. He was one of the organizers of the parent tailgate party and was dressed head to toe in Purple and Red—a true Wildcat fan. His decorated trailer was the tailgating centerpiece with its massive spread of food and drinks.

I introduced myself and asked the first questions every tailgating parent asks, "Who is your son, what is his number, and what position does he play?"

His answer stunned me, "Oh, my son doesn't play on the team anymore. He couldn't maintain his grades to stay eligible. He **retired** two years ago."

Wha-wha-what? Retired?

What did I just hear? Did I hear the word "retire"?

Really?

Hold on one second. This young man refused to do the work required to earn the privilege of playing for the team with the longest winning season streak in college football history. He is **ineligible** to play football, but this parent called it "retirement"?

Can you hear the lawnmower's two-stroke engine buzzing in the background? I can.

Later that day I Googled the word and here's what I found: "to leave one's job and cease to work, typically upon reaching the **normal age** for leaving employment."

I've heard this word used to describe quitting a half a dozen times since by the generation that invented the Participation Trophy. It's the new buzzword among quitters. We should be ashamed. What's wrong with us? What have we become? When will we accept responsibility for our actions and the actions of those we love?

Call it what it is. Quitting. Stop pacifying the throw-in-the-towel mentality that has hit epidemic proportions and start holding people accountable for their actions! Here's a suggestion.

Throw obstacles in the way of your children. Let the lawn grow. Let the dirt pile up. Show **them** how to use a bulldozer, teach them how to mow the lawn, and get out of the seat. Watch **them** knock down every obstacle in their way with guts, determination, and perseverance. Coach them when they fail. They will. At least give them the chance

Colton loves Toyota 4Runners. He owned three by the time he was twenty-two. When he bought his first one, I warned him about buying a car with over two-hundred thousand miles on it, and that he should look for one with lower miles. But he had to have it, and a few months later the transmission went out. Without four thousand dollars to have a professional replace it, he pulled one off a wreck and replaced it himself. It took him and his buddies **four times** to finally get it right. But he did. He's wiser, more experienced, and a better man for it. I was so proud of him.

Obstacles are a part of life. It's what we do with them that either strengthens or weakens our character. Let's look at a man who refused to be broken down by life's unforeseen obstacles.

Unbroken

Louie Zamperini (1917-2014) was a winner, not a whiner. He was a finisher. He was one of the strongest men our country has produced, but it came at a great price. He knew how to persevere under fire. Zamperini qualified for the Olympics in the 5000-meter race and competed in the 1936 Olympics in Berlin, Germany, where he finished eighth place.

In 1941, he joined the United States Air Force as a Lieutenant and served as a bombardier on a B-24 Liberator in the Pacific. On a search and rescue mission, Zamperini's plane crashed in the Pacific Ocean due to mechanical failure. After drifting at sea for 47 days, he landed on the Japanese occupied Marshall Islands where he was promptly captured, taken to a prison camp in Japan, and repeatedly tortured. The character, courage, and determination of Zamperini are brilliantly portrayed in the 2014 biographical movie, **Unbroken**. I highly recommend you watch his epic story of survival under the worst of conditions.

Later in life, Zamperini made a powerful statement that we could apply to both sports and life, "That's one thing you learn in sports. You don't give up; you fight to the finish."

I'm inspired by a life like this. We all are. Strong men model their lives after other men who live an authentic life as the best—most courageous—version of themselves. To weaker men who have watched the movie, Zamperini's life seems surreal and unattainable. The truth of his life seems out of reach to so many. His strength and resolve are portrayals of some sort of fictional comic book hero that is opposite to so many in our generation who retire early, refuse to fight to the bitter end, and just quit.

But his life stands as a model for those with the tenacity to fight hard and finish strong. A life like that stands out in the sea of anonymous men who find comfort from the safety of the bleachers and refuse to enter the arena. Or worse, who have experienced a taste of the blood, sweat, and tears that strong masculinity requires and opted not to continue down that road.

Paper Fire

Some men burn out. Others rust out. Still others slowly fade out. But the results are the same—leaving the risk of the arena for the safety of the bleachers, they quit.

The Quitter is easy to spot in the crowd. Finishers can smell their decaying stench from miles away. They wordsmith **quitting** to disguise their true character because, deep down, they are ashamed of the weak male they've become. When in a mixed crowd of men, they'll masquerade as men, but their own words quickly betray them. It's easy to condemn the Quitter. It's much tougher to reform him, which is the goal of strong men. The weak man, the Quitter, may need you to carry him back into the game until he is strong enough to stand on his own. Listen to what Galatians 6: 1-5 teaches:

> *"Brethren, even if anyone is caught in any trespass, you who*
> *are spiritual, restore such a one in a spirit of gentleness; each*
> *one looking to yourself, so that you too will not be tempted.*
> *Bear one another's burdens, and thereby fulfill the law of*
> *Christ. For if anyone thinks he is something when he is*
> *nothing, he deceives himself. But each one must examine his*
> *own work, and then he will have reason for boasting in regard*
> *to himself alone, and not in regard to another. For each one*
> *will bear his own load."*

It's a stronger man's obligation not to condemn but to encourage. That being said, here are the signs of a Quitter.

He has a history of making excuses for quitting. He wordsmiths quitting into something less potent, even spiritual, like resign, retire or, "God is moving him on". In fact, he often projects his quitting onto God by making statements like, "God called me out. God led me. God put a new thing on my heart." Jesus modeled a spirit of grit, determination and strength leading up to the cross and beyond. Jesus is our ultimate example of manhood who,

> *"For the joy set before Him endured the cross, despising the shame, and has sat down at the right hand of the throne of God. For consider Him who has endured such hostility by sinners against Himself, so that you will not grow weary and lose heart. You have not yet resisted to the point of shedding blood in your striving against sin" (Hebrews 12:2-4).*

It's troubling that so many seminary trained professional ministers lack the biblical virtue of endurance that Jesus modeled, resign at the hint of conflict, and blame it all on some mysterious calling from God. "How will this man lift a weaker man onto his shoulders, when he is burdened and shackled with the same weakness?"

Another sign of a Quitter is that he supports others when they surrender to attrition, because he knows his history will soon repeat itself too. He lives a transient lifestyle. His roots are shallow in his family, career, community, and church. He's known by some but not known well because his roots are shallow and uprooted often. He is often a jack of all trades but master of none. He's done a lot. His resume is full. But he's done nothing for very long, well, or with a lasting impact.

He's a paper fire. Like paper his life is dry and has no fuel to burn over time.

He makes a great first impression. He's mastered the art of the first impression because he knows his lasting impression will be an epic fail. He has yet to learn that his *last* impression will be his *lasting* impression. Beware of the man who comes on hard and fast, seeking immediate position, power, or popularity.

He is tough to resist, especially in churches where our staffing needs are so great. I cannot caution you enough that when you spot a Quitter, put him on your shoulders by slowing any promotion to a crawl. Save him from himself and those that will be hurt by trusting him.

He burns hot and fast like a blazing paper fire, but he'll burn down just as fast. Avoid giving instant authority to any man seeking fast power. Make him prove his long-term value, and that he isn't a paper fire.

I was speaking on this topic at a men's weekend, when one man stood up and confessed, "Your Paper Fire List describes me. I'm a Quitter. I've always been a Quitter. I need help!"

Confessing the sin of quitting was the first step to healing for this man. Calling **yourself** out in front of those you trust is the first step in blazing a new trial as a Finisher. Make that the first step. Determine that you will live as a new man, a Finisher. Persevere with strong finishes one day at a time compounded over a lifetime and become the best version of you.

Strengthen Your Grip
Small Group Exercise

What stood out the most out to you when you read the locker room quote, "A quitter never wins. A winner never quits?" Share about a struggle that caused you to consider quitting.

In 2 Timothy 4:7 the apostle Paul wrote, "I have fought the good fight, I have finished the course, I have kept the faith." Which of these three are you battling the hardest to do?

Louis Zamperini, "I'd made it this far and refused to give up because all my life I had always finished the race." How do you apply this to your life?

Jim wrote, "Some men burn out. Others rust out. Still others slowly fade out. But the results are the same, leaving the risk of arena for the safety of the bleachers, they quit." What does a Paper Fire look like and how can you be sure to never be that guy?

FINISH TODAY STRONG
Strong Finishes Compound Over Time

"Let's put it on the table. If you're not teachable, you don't have a chance in the world of finishing strong. Not a chance."
~ Steve Farrar: Finishing Strong

The end of a matter is better than its beginning.
~Ecclesiastes 7:8

"He who has never failed cannot be great. Failure is the true test of greatness."
~Herman Melville

Short

Robert Southey (1774-1843) was an English poet who once wrote, "It is with words as with sunbeams. The more they are condensed, the deeper they burn."

This chapter is strategically shorter than the rest because I want to sear it into your heart and mind. It's so impactful—so life changing—I don't want you to lose it amidst words that might drown the resounding sound of what you must know.

It doesn't matter how old or young you are, finishing strong must become the goal of every **man**. Let this chapter burn into the depths of your soul.

First, I need to tell you about my ugly cousin.

My Ugly Cousin

While living he was known as the ugliest man to ever hold a high political office. He had the equivalent to vertical cross-eyes, was color blind, and had a long-term problem with corns on his feet that were so painful he could barely wear shoes. In the more prominent pictures we have of him, he's wearing a jacket and hat because he had unusually thin skin and was often very cold.

. . .

My ugly, now dead cousin had a long list of defeats and failures but overcame them all to finish strong.

- At **22** his business failed.
- At **23** he was defeated as a candidate for the state legislature.
- At **twenty-four** he experienced another business failure.
- But he experienced his first win at only **25** years old when he was elected to the state legislature.
- Then, at **26** years old the love of his life died tragically, and at **27** he had a nervous breakdown.
- At age **29** he lost the race for Speaker of the House.
- When he was **31**, he was defeated again as Elector for the Electoral College.
- At **34** he was beaten again in his campaign for the U.S. Congress. Will my ugly cousin ever give up? No, a few years later he was beaten again when he lost the race for Congress at **37** years old and lost again at age **39**.
- At **46** he ran for a seat in the Senate—and lost—of course. His track record of winning was so high (I'm being sarcastic), that he ran for Vice-President of the United States of America, which he did at **47** years old, and lost—again.
- At **49** he was defeated in another race for the U.S. Senate.
- But at **51** he was elected as the **16th** President of the United States of America, President Abraham Lincoln!

He might have been the ugliest man to ever hold a high political office, but he was arguably the greatest President the United States of America has ever seen.

I'm proud to be the distant cousin of a man who refused to give up. I might be a little ugly myself, don't tell Shanna, because I've convinced her that I'm the best-looking dude in America!

A couple years ago, I had the privilege to visit the Lincoln Presidential Library and Museum in Springfield, Illinois, and was blown away at how difficult Lincoln's life actually was.

Can you imagine the extreme stress of leading our country through the bloodiest war ever fought on American soil, The Civil War? In the Museum, named in his honor, is the display of Lincoln's "Death Mask". It's a plaster mold taken of Lincoln during the Civil War. It's called the Death Mask because Lincoln had aged so much from the stress of the war that one expert referred to it as, "The face of a man who was dead, though living."

Another fact we don't hear about was that of his four sons only one lived past age 18. He mourned the death of a son on **three separate occasions**!

His wife, Mary, suffered from severe headaches throughout her adult life, and was often depressed. Her history of mood swings, fierce temper, and public outbursts throughout Lincoln's presidency, as well as excessive spending, has led some historians and psychologists to speculate that Mary suffered from bipolar disorder. She was **involuntarily** institutionalized by her one living son for psychiatric disease, 10 years after her husband's assassination.

What a remarkable, yet tragic, story of a man who lived a hard life, fought for every inch of ground, and had his life cut tragically short. But his life continues to impact lives today. Abraham Lincoln overcame failure after failure and finished his life strong.

Yesterday

"What's the first (and most crucial?) step to finish strong when you've had plenty of practice at finishing wrong?" My answer may surprise you. I've spent many hours thinking and discussing the topic and here is the conviction I hold about strong finishers.

First, forget your past. It's gone. It's over. You can't get it back. Some of you don't want it back. You're ashamed. You're embarrassed. You have regrets. I know. We all do.

One of my favorite quotes came from another great finisher, Apostle Paul who wrote, *"But one thing I do: forgetting what lies behind and reaching forward to what lies ahead, I press on toward the goal for the prize" (Philippians 3:13-14).*

Listen to these great words. Forget the past, and what lies behind you. Stop dwelling on it. Reach forward. Press on. Follow God's great mission selected just for you!

Forgive yourself every day until you actually do. Starts aren't nearly as important as finishes. I've learned that no matter how bad your failure is in the public eye; people forget about it and move on after about a month. Why don't you? There's nothing of value back there. Live as your best version, learn from your mistakes, and move on to become the man you're created to be.

Today

Second, you are the sum of your choices and the choices of others. These choices, compounded over time, become your life. Do you want to finish life strong? Here's how.

Find a pen and highlight this—circle it. I'm keeping it short. Dog-ear this page. Put a bookmark here. Memorize it! Create an alert on your smartphone. Here it is in bold letters:

Finish today strong. Then, finish tomorrow strong. Repeat this every day for the rest of your life. When you do this day after day, month after month, and year after year, it will compound to a strong life finish—YOUR strong life finish.

Tomorrow

Let me articulate. You have a job. You work hard. You're up first every day and last to bed every night. You come home tired. You've zeroed your word count, work hours, and the waking minutes of your day. You are exhausted. You live in the Stress Bubble, where men are thrown into this new arena of raising a family, loving one woman, working hard at a job, and serving their community.

Many are ill prepared. Over 40% are caught off guard by an unplanned pregnancy and thrust into the furnace like Meshach, Shadrach, and Abed-nego (Daniel 3:19-23). Many had no father to lead the way. Many are left to figure it out on their own.

Strong men are forged in the fires of the Stress Bubble. Weaker men are broken. Nothing demands more of a man than this 25-year period we call the Stress Bubble—that we also call the Arena.

During that season nothing sounds better than throwing yourself in the recliner, popping a cold one, and grabbing the remote control. Every day, he faces the temptation to put it on cruise control, rest, and relax until bedtime. I remember **begging** Shanna for just 20 minutes before engaging with three wild boys who had been waiting all day for daddy, and an exhausted wife who had been speaking toddler for the past ten hours, anticipating when she can finally have an adult conversation.

That is why every man in the arena is a hero.

You're a man. You're a strong one. You're a different strong species than a weaker, softer, male. More than that, you're a man who finishes each day strong.

So you put down the remote and pick up one of those children hanging on your leg. Stop playing video games and play with your children instead. Get off the couch and get out to coach your child's amoeba soccer team. Get the drink out of your hands and hold your woman instead.

You get the point. Your family needs you to suck it up and be strong for them. You are tired. But they need your best, and not your cold leftovers. That 6:00-9:00 PM window is the **most important part** of your day, every day for the hero of his family.

What you do in that time frame, compounded over time, is the line of demarcation between finishing strong and finishing wrong. It's also the line between strength and weakness.

I guarantee it.

Too many men end their life with untapped potential. My Stepfather left this earth with a question mark. Others leave with a comma. Some leave with an ellipsis (…). Good men might leave with a period, but is that your goal?

No. You want to leave as the best version of yourself and a hero to those who love you most.

Steve Farrar, in his book *Finishing Strong* wrote, "It takes vision to finish strong." So dream big! Leave with something better. Finish like the ultimate Alpha Man: Jesus! Make it your goal to end your life with an exclamation mark!

Strengthen Your Grip
Small Group Exercise

In Ecclesiastes 7:8, Solomon wrote "The end of a matter is better than its beginning." This was strategically the shortest chapter in the book. Why?

Herman Melville wrote, "He who has never failed cannot be great. Failure is the true test of greatness." Why is failure so important in forming the masculine character trait of finishing strong?

In Philippians 3:13-14 a great finisher, the Apostle Paul, wrote, "But one thing I do: forgetting what lies behind and reaching forward to what lies ahead, I press on toward the goal for the prize." How can your past hinder your future? What past failures are hindering you from becoming your best version?

Jim concluded this short chapter with a powerful equation: "Finish today strong. Then, finish tomorrow strong. Repeat this every day for the rest of your life. When you do this day after day, month after month, and year after year, it will compound to a strong life finish—YOUR strong life finish." What does this look like in your life?

EXCLAMATION MARK
Weary, Whine, or War Cry?

"A man can travel 7,000 miles around the world, but it's the last thirty inches that really matter."
~Don Owens

This is what the Lord of Heaven's Armies says:
"Be strong and finish the task!"
~Zechariah 8:9 (NLT)

"It's hard to beat a person who never gives up."
~Babe Ruth

Eight Semester Rule

When I was living in California, I heard a hilarious, yet troubling, story about the Valedictorian of a large local high school. The newspaper recorded his ingenious senior prank that started after the Valedictorian-to-be found a loophole in the Valedictorian requirements.

The class Valedictorian was selected each year upon completion of their seventh (of eight) semesters. This gave him or her time to prepare their graduation speech, get approval from administration, and receive editing advice from select teachers. Once the Valedictorian decision was determined, it was final.

The mischievous Valedictorian decided to do something unprecedented during his eighth semester.

Nothing.

That's right. He purposely failed every class, and by the time the administration caught on to his devious prank the graduation ceremony was over, and his speech had been delivered!

True story.

By the time school was back in session, the Eight Semester Rule was implemented! The young man in question finished with all the accolades of being class Valedictorian but finished wrong nonetheless.

Alpha Man and Finishing Strong

The Valedictorian in our story is very unlike what my friend and the author of *Defending the Feminine Heart*, Jeff Voth, calls the ultimate Alpha man. Jesus not only called himself the Alpha but the Omega as well; *"I am the Alpha and the Omega, the first and the last, the beginning and the end" (Revelation 22:13).*

Churches today have turned this ultimate Alpha man into some soft and tender Savior who spends his days holding sheep and hugging children. Although it's true that He did those things, this is still the same man who violently expelled a crowd of retailers from the Jerusalem temple grounds and called his three closest friends the Sons of Thunder and the Rock!

Even on the cross, Jesus is often wrongly portrayed as some anguished Savior who we should feel sorry for, but more on that later. Let's examine Jesus and his thoughts about finishing. He was a man on a mission. He knew exactly why He had come and what He had to do. What did Jesus have to say about finishing?

Jesus counted the cost and knew what that meant for His life: *"For which one of you, when he wants to build a tower, does not first sit down and calculate the cost to see if he has enough **to complete** it? Otherwise, when he has laid a foundation and is not able to finish, all who observe it begin to ridicule him" (Luke 14:28-29).*

Not only was He willing but hungry to finish what He started: *"My food,"* said Jesus, *"is to do the will of him who sent me and to **finish** his work" (John 4:34—NIV).*

One chapter later Jesus speaks again about His deep desire to finish the mission: *"For the very work that the Father has given me to **finish**, and which I am doing, testifies that the Father has sent me" (John 5:36—NIV).*

To call myself a follower of the ultimate man, Jesus, means I will follow Him into everything He leads me to experience. I will follow Him to victory. I will follow Him in loss. I will follow Him to pleasure. I will follow Him to pain. I will follow Him with all the strength left in me and, God willing, will finish each glorious endeavor just as He did.

Jesus always finished strong.

So will I.

Asphyxiation

What was Jesus' mission? What task did He come to finish? The best answer came from Jesus himself who summed up his life's mission in *Luke 19:10*, *"For the Son of Man has come to seek and to save that which was lost."*

He knew it would cost His life, but He did it anyway. He must have known how He would die as well. Death by crucifixion was a horrible death and the Romans had perfected it. Ultimately it was death by asphyxiation.

Everett Harrison in his book, *A Short Life of Christ* writes, "Even for a callous age, crucifixion was a cruel punishment." As the cross was dropped in the ground, the shoulders would be dislocated on impact. This would lower the body below the lungs and the only way to breathe was to raise the body up by driving the feet down on the nail hammered through the feet. Jesus did this for three hours, after being beaten and flogged, with a crown of thorns puncturing his skull.

Imagine that day with me for a moment. Jesus' mission is minutes away from fulfillment. All his life had led Him to this point.

He knew his life on this dark planet was close to its end. The hole in his feet was loose and wide, his flesh worn from hours of driving his body upward using the nail as his morbid brace. His breathing was more labored now than ever and Jesus sensed a single breath left in his lungs.

He saw the thundering death clouds beginning to form in the sky above. Maybe He heard the rocks beginning to crack and the earth starting to shake. Maybe He sensed the very fabric of the temple curtain that veiled the Holy of Holies begin to tear under divine stress.

It was now or never.

In that final moment his senses were heightened greater than any other moment on this planet and He knew the time was now. His final breath would be his best. He would finish strong.

He had one last mark to leave for all who would follow Him. Would it be a comma, question mark, or a semicolon? No, not today, and not ever.

By now the crude spike of a nail ripped the mangled flesh in his feet and was so loose it could barely support his broken body. The mock crown of thorns was embedded deep into the back of his skull and pulled almost over his blackened eyes from hours of elevating his body to breathe. The splinters of the vertical beam were most likely worn deeply into his flogged and brutally exposed flesh.

The holes in his wrists were so badly maimed that if it weren't for the ropes around his arms, He'd flail wildly to steady himself.

The crowd watched in wonder.

"Is He dead yet?" someone asked.

He pushed upward one final time.

"No! Wait! He isn't dead. Look! He's moving. He is lifting himself up for another breath!"

Jesus struggled, a life and death struggle, for one more, one final gasp of air.

It was His last chance to make a proclamation for the universe to hear, the exclamation of his mission to save the human race. He ignored the splinters driving into his raw back and the thorns penetrating deeper into his skull and neck. He ignored the sting of his own blood in his eyes and his mangled hands and feet where the nails were driven into his wrists and ankles. He pushed his body upward.

And He pushed.

He pushed with the resolve that would make the greatest of warriors envious. He pushed on, up, and up on that bloody vertical beam until He could feel his lungs expand for one final gasp.

It would be his last.

The crowd stopped jeering. Stopped mocking. Some stopped breathing themselves, caught in the awe and wonder of the moment. The soldiers stopped gambling for his clothes. The mockers stopped mocking. All watched and listened.

In one moment all of eternity was silent... perfect...still...

All eyes were fixed on the man, the underdog—Jesus. The weight of the sins of the world weighed Him down yet as He pushed down, upward his body lifted for the last time. The hearts of even those who hated Him silently rooted Him upward. Up He drove his body, higher, then higher.

Slowly, purposely He opened His broken mouth. In that moment the grimace on his beaten face turned into a smile and in his dying breath... He screamed a war cry like none before or ever after.

"IT...IS...FINNISSSSSSSSSHHHHHHHHHHHED!" (John 19:30).

And He bowed his head and gave up his spirit. How he finished that day, for me, is everything. The exclamation mark is everything.

The problem is that too many of us don't live for the exclamation mark. We live timidly. We die anonymously. We retire and fade away. We tap out. We throw in the towel. We quit just shy of the war cry. We end short of the victory chant.

But not Jesus. He pushed through the pain to the exclamation mark.

A Problem

There's one problem with my interpretation of Jesus' finish. The ancient Hebrew language does not use vowels or punctuation marks. Similarly, neither of the Aramaic and Greek languages used punctuation marks. We either have to figure this out on our own or be subject to the interpretations of theologians. To keep it simple and straightforward, I'll limit my research to those translations that use exclamation marks in John 19:30.

You won't see the exclamation mark if your Bible is: English Standard Version, New International Version, King James Version, The Message, American Standard Version, New Revised Standard Version, Wycliffe, or Darby translations (sorry son).

But if your Bible is one of the following, you'll be excited to see an exclamation mark prominently displayed. Personally, I refused to spend time or money on Bible translations that neglect the exclamation mark on John 19:30.

Yes, it's that important to me.

Here are some translations that include it: New American Standard (NASB was used in this book unless noted), The Voice, New Living Translation, **New King James**, Contemporary English Version, JB Phillips, and the Hawaiian Pidgin:

> "Wen Jesus wen suck da cheap wine he say, 'Every ting pau awready!' An he wen bend down his head, an den let go his spirit."

I love it! One reason the exclamation mark was included (besides what I read about Jesus the man in Scripture) is that the Gospel of John is the only gospel that **does not** mention Jesus crying out from the cross. But John is the only one that includes the statement "It is finished!". I believe the others were referring to, "It is finished!" when they mention Jesus crying out. Here they are for your interpretation and understanding:

And Jesus **cried out again** with a loud voice, and yielded up His
  spirit.
  ~Matthew 27:50

And Jesus **cried out again** with a loud voice, and yielded up His
  spirit.
  ~Mark 15:37

And Jesus, **crying out** with a loud voice, said, "Father, into Your
  hands I commit My spirit." Having said this, He breathed His
  last.
  ~Luke 23:46

Based on the accounts in Matthew, Mark, and John I don't flinch one bit when
reading Luke's account but would add, "It is finished!" to Luke 23:46 to read
what I believe Jesus actually said: *"And Jesus, crying out with a loud voice, said,
"Father, into Your hands I commit My spirit." Having said (this), **"It is
finished!"** He breathed His last.*

Simple. It's not complicated.

Options

Commentator William Barclay writes, "Jesus died with a shout of triumph on
his lips. He did not say, 'It is finished,' in weary defeat; He said it as one who
shouts for joy because the victory was won."

Although passionate about the exclamation mark, I acknowledge that there
are other options out there, especially with those Bible translations that leave the
exclamation mark out. Based on those exclusionary translations let me give you
three options when considering how Jesus finished on the cross.

We live in a world of options. We live in a world that even has options about
who Jesus was based on our interpretations of the Bible. Here they are.

. . .

Option #1: Jesus died with a weary cry of relief because his suffering was finally over.

In other words, Jesus', "It is finished!" was a loud moan and not a war cry. Psalm 90:9 says, *"All our days pass away under your wrath; we finish our years with a moan" (NIV)*. Jesus suffered a horrific death. After hours of torturous treatment, he died with a weary cry on his lips. This seems to be the most popular interpretation of what happened, by the media and more popular Bible translations. Based on my decades of experience in the local church, this makes the most sense. It's wrong of course, but it makes sense that people would believe this option.

Option #2: Jesus died with a wimpy cry of anguish because his ministry was an epic failure.

If you're reading this and haven't surrendered your life to the ultimate man and Savior of the World, Jesus the Messiah, then you may believe this interpretation. Why wouldn't you?

But this is an impossible option for myself or any follower of Jesus to accept. Too much has happened since to accept this option as credible on any level. Years ago, I was impacted by the anonymous poem, *One Solitary Life* by James Allen (1926). It's convincing. Here it is.

- He was born in an obscure village
- The child of a peasant woman
- He grew up in another obscure village
- Where he worked in a carpenter shop until he was thirty
- He never wrote a book
- He never held an office
- He never went to college
- He never visited a big city
- He never travelled more than two hundred miles
- From the place where he was born
- He did none of the things
- Usually associated with greatness
- He had no credentials but himself
- He was only thirty-three
- His friends ran away
- One of them denied him

- He was turned over to his enemies
- And went through the mockery of a trial
- He was nailed to a cross between two thieves
- While dying, his executioners gambled for his clothing
- The only property he had on earth
- When he was dead
- He was laid in a borrowed grave
- Through the pity of a friend
- Nineteen centuries have come and gone
- And today Jesus is the central figure of the human race
- And the leader of mankind's progress
- All the armies that have ever marched
- All the navies that have ever sailed
- All the parliaments that have ever sat
- All the kings that ever reigned put together
- Have not affected the life of mankind on earth
- As powerfully as that one solitary life

Many of Jesus' contemporaries, including Saul of Tarsus, later known as the Apostle Paul, might have mistakenly thought it was a wimpy cry of defeat, but this couldn't be further from the truth. His miraculous birth, resurrection from the dead, and the endurance of His Church are proof that this option isn't viable.

Option #3: Jesus died with a war cry of victory because God had triumphed, changing the course of history!

According to *The Discovery Bible* (a New American Standard Bible translation), the verb form of *finished* literally means: "It is finished and now still is still finished. It's an action whose results or effects go on; an action leaving a *condition or state* of lasting significance or status."

Wow. The wording is difficult at first but still powerful. What do you believe about Jesus' last words? Better yet, what do you believe about Jesus?

Your Mark on This World

Jesus did it on the cross. We did it with this book. Both were finished with exclamation marks. The only question left is, how will you finish today, then tomorrow, and every day after?

. . .

The three finish-on-the-cross options of Jesus are also available for your life too. Will your life finish with a **weary cry of relief** because it's finally over for you? Will you retire into oblivion and anonymity like most men today? Will you coast? Will you be a non-contributor to the greater good of humanity?

Or, will you finish with a wimpy cry of anguish because your life was an epic fail? You wanted a do-over but realized too late that it wasn't an option. You've lived with regrets you've never forgiven yourself for, broken relationships you never made right, and potential you never used, all because you weren't strong enough to do the next right thing and move on to victory.

The things you devoted your life to are worthless in the context of eternity just as Peter wrote about, *"In this you greatly rejoice, even though now for a little while, if necessary, you have been distressed by various trials, so that the proof of your faith, being more precious than gold which is perishable, even though* **tested by fire***, may be found to result in praise and glory and honor at the revelation of Jesus Christ"* (1 Peter 1:6-7).

If you continue on this path much longer, your life will not have mattered the way God designed it. You won't be missed long after you're gone.

Worse yet, what if after you die you realize that the eternal life with God in heaven you assumed would be yours, is not available for you? You called yourself a "Christian" but never committed your life to Him? You knew a lot about God but never actually knew Him. You never took the trouble to follow Him with your life, surrendering to Him as your Savior. You refused to live in preparation for this moment, and now you're screwed. You never lived in relationship with the Savior who died that brutal death for the very purpose of making you fully prepared for when this moment hits, and now it's too late (Hebrews 9:27).

Will you cry in futile **anguish** at that moment?

But it's not too late to change. It's not over until it's over.

Or will you, like the thousands upon thousands who will read this book, take option three, a **bold cry of victory**? Will you live from this day forth to finish with a war cry of victory because you fought hard and finished strong?

One day you'll swing your last sword in life's arena. Bloodied and scarred from battle, you boldly fought in the arena of life, and won. After your last war cry you'll come face to face with a dark-skinned, thick-armed, and broad-smiled man who'll pull you off the arena floor, stare into your eyes, and say those words you've lived to hear, *"Well done, good and faithful servant. You were faithful with a few things, I will put you in charge of many things; enter into the joy of your master" (Matthew 25:23).*

Oh, how I long to hear those words! Even now, tears in my eyes, I long to hear those words.

Exclamation

I promised to end this book with an exclamation mark and here we are. This is the battle cry of the book. This is the end of a book but the beginning in your new life as a man in the arena. Some of you, in the pages of this book, have thrown off your male shell and stepped into your best version. You are committed to be the hero for your family and a champion in God's story. We are so excited for you and are here to guide you through life's many obstacles.

Some will, sadly, place this book on a shelf, walk away, and continue down the weak and worn path of those anonymous faces that refuse to leave the nameless bleachers. They are life's greatest tragedy.

Others, already strong, will answer the call to action just as they have for years. They are the true heroes of this story. In the arena of manhood, they battle for the best version of their brothers. They carry the weak. Guide the lost. Mend the broken. Protect the helpless. Cover the naked. They fight the wicked. They rise to every challenge because they aren't just men.

They are strong men!

Strengthen Your Grip

Small Group Exercise

What are the Five Essentials discussed in this book? Is there one that particularly stands out to you? Why?

Why is Don Owens' quote, "A man can travel 7,000 miles around the world, but it's the last thirty inches that really matter," so vital for the man who desires a strong life finish?

In the New Living Translation of Zechariah 8:9 we read, "This is what the Lord of Heaven's Armies says: 'Be strong and finish the task!'" Why is it so important for a strong finish?

John is the only Gospel writer to include Jesus' "It is finished!" war cry (John 19:30). The other three Gospels record that Jesus "Cried out with a loud voice" before giving up his spirit (Matthew 27:50, Mark 15:37, and Luke 23:46). How do you interpret John 19:30 in view of these facts?

What punctuation does your Bible have after John 19:30? If there is no exclamation mark, consider the Men in the Arena *Life Essentials Bible* by Gene Getz as a great tool in your masculine arsenal. The *Life Essentials Bible* has 1500 videos explaining major portions of Scripture. You can pick up your copy at www.meninthearena.org.

ACKNOWLEDGMENTS

This book wouldn't be possible if it weren't for several key men and women who worked tirelessly to produce this high-quality book. *Strong Men Dangerous Times*, is published by Five Stones Press.

I also want to thank my writing coach, friend, and editor, Ken Watson. Ken's tenacity and brutal honesty is exactly what I needed. This book would be less than excellent without him. Thanks Ken!

Thanks to my wonderful Executive Assistant, Sammie Farmer, who keeps me on task and was a major player in the editing process.

I also want to thank my copy editors and proofreaders. These volunteers worked diligently to return each draft section promptly and accurately. Thank you, Carla Schrock, Lori Cutrel, and Emilie Strong. This project wouldn't have been be possible without you.

ABOUT THE AUTHOR

I've been married to my best friend Shanna since 1992. She's the most important person in my life and my best friend. We love drinking coffee, traveling to Tropical places, and eating out with friends.

I'm an avid book reader, love the great outdoors, but my real passion is hunting. My sons are my hunting partners along with a few select men. I love hanging out with men over a cup of good coffee and learning their story. You can learn more about my story at meninthearena.org

In 2012 we founded Men in the Arena with the deep conviction to trust Jesus Christ to build an army of men who are becoming the best version of themselves in Christ and changing their world.

Because when a man gets it—everyone wins!

Join our army today and let us help you become your best version and hero to those you love. Thank you so much for spending your valuable time with this book.

f **◎**

Made in the USA
Columbia, SC
01 August 2021

42805338R00115